Deep Encounters

Steps toward Dissolving the 21st Century Mystery and Discovering the Truly Global Learner

Permeated with and Enhanced by a
"genuine introduction to Japanese culture"

Eiji Hattori and Wallace Gray

University Press of America,® Inc.
Lanham · Boulder · New York · Toronto · Plymouth, UK

Copyright © 2009 by
University Press of America,® Inc.
4501 Forbes Boulevard
Suite 200
Lanham, Maryland 20706
UPA Acquisitions Department (301) 459-3366

Estover Road
Plymouth PL6 7PY
United Kingdom

All rights reserved
Printed in the United States of America
British Library Cataloging in Publication Information Available

Library of Congress Control Number: 2009927842
ISBN-13: 978-0-7618-4695-6 (clothbound : alk. paper)
ISBN-10: 0-7618-4695-6 (clothbound : alk. paper)
ISBN-13: 978-0-7618-4586-7 (paperback : alk. paper)
ISBN-10: 0-7618-4586-0 (paperback : alk. paper)
eISBN-13: 978-0-7618-4587-4
eISBN-10: 0-7618-4587-9

∞™ The paper used in this publication meets the minimum
requirements of American National Standard for Information
Sciences—Permanence of Paper for Printed Library Materials,
ANSI Z39.48-1992

Contents

Preface	vii
Acknowledgements	ix
Eiji Hattori and the Firefly – Wallace Gray's Introduction	xi
Part I. Deep Encounters	1
1. Buddhas of Chartres	3
A Deep Encounter	
2. Water *Is* Life	8
Thinking with the Mediterranean Poet Paul Valéry	
3. To Be or To Appear	12
Remembering Jean-Louis Barrault	
4. Being and Having	17
Learning from Gabriel Marcel	
5. The Logic of the City	22
kō ("official") and *kōkyō* ("public")	
6. The Light of Reason	27
Descartes and Noah's Ark	
7. An Apocalyptic World	32
Now it's time to think about Kant	
8. The Holy Mother Ascends	37
The Sea and Life	
9. Earth's Dignity	42
Visiting Greece in the Springtime	
10. "Quo Vadis, Domine?"	46
People Who Have Seen God	
11. Way to China	51
The Route Napoleon Lost	
12. Writing the Future	55
Kaii Higashiyama's Memorable Poster, "The Road"	
Part II. Words That Are Ensouled	59
13. Japan	61
A Country with "Soul-Filled" Words	
14. What is the Form of Japan?	66
Concerning the Feminine Principle	

Contents

15.	Freedom and Nature Learning from Daisetsu Suzuki	71
16.	The Hidden Being Monotheism and Polytheism	76
17.	A Bird Calls, Then the Mountain Deepens Its Silence Reflections in a Tea Pavilion	81
18.	The Encounter of a Lifetime What Rikyū Found	86
19.	Rationale for the Elimination of Collectivism Concerning the Culture of Shame	91
20.	Families with No Alpha Figure Dynamics of a Boy's Crime	96
21.	Educating People to Think for Themselves Good Uses for "Useless" Leisure	101
22.	Searching for Lost Times The Last Words of Emperor Showa (1926-1989)	106

Part III. The Tree of Life — 111

23.	Love and Indifference What I Saw in Bombay	113
24.	Under the Baobab Tree Reflecting on Democracy	117
25.	The Tree of Life Climbing the Symbiotic Line	122
26.	Stories of Deities From the Soul of the Ainu People	127
27.	The Tragedy of Easter Island A Warning from Jacques Cousteau	131
28.	Churning the Sea of Milk Decline and Creation	135
29.	Land of Gods in the Himalayas Finding Unexpected Angels Deep in the Mountains	140
30.	Black Skies An Unexpected Attack from Yellow Sands	145
31.	The Mountain Sees Rihaku Images That Move the Mind Toward Quantum Theory	149
32.	Night Thoughts Occasioned by a Falling Star Causality (因, IN) and Supercausality (縁, EN)	154

Contents

Part IV. The Ultimate Glow: Pulling It All Together 159

33. Japan for the World 161
    Noh Theater as Change-Agent in the 21st Century
34. UNESCO for the World 164
    Controversy and Movement
35. USA for the World 167
    Humility and Arrogance
36. A Holistic Philosophy for Each and All 172
    Towards Transcultural Dialogue

The Authors 183

Preface
by Eiji Hattori

> I remember the white sun of Scandinavia that waits and waits to finally sink. But the true "white night" is in Paris under roofs that lie beneath the dark blue sky before the dawn creeps in to cover the sleepless town.[1]

These words popped up among some fragmentary jottings of mine from my late twenties. It seems to me that this scrap of writing still conveys my thoughts and feelings at that time. I remember these nights tasting mildly bitter. I spent one whole night muttering to myself the Latin proverb *Ars longa, vita brevis* – "While life is too short, study takes a long time" – as if the proverb gave an excuse to me.

When I consider the matter, my own life has been full of twists and turns, including surprise encounters that have always helped me stay on the right track. Precisely because of my encounters with so many people I have felt at times to be almost drawn aloft. The invisible and mysterious power to see the convergence of my different experiences of encounter may be aptly described by the Japanese term *en* meaning here, "invisible thread."[2]

The route I traced through life may be described as a chain of encounters – encounters with the parents who brought me up, with the many teachers who guided me, and with the ideas that propelled me to heights and insights beyond the ordinary. My encounters were not limited to people. There were the flowers whispering in the sunlight of Greece, the endless Desert of Death in Western China, the purity of nature as observed in the interior of Africa, the oceans changing their colors constantly every day and every night, the white peaks among the Himalayan mountain dwellings of the gods, the murmuring of limpid valley streams in Japan, the atmosphere of mystery in high mountains and deep valleys, the stone-paved roads of Paris where a fairy called Love played, the scenes of human love facing misery's sorrow on earth, and the radiant brightness in the eyes of children the world over . . . .

When I think carefully about it, my "self" is nothing but a focus of these memories and my personhood is none other than a point of convergence of such

---

1. Here in the author's reminiscence, "white night" is used as in the French expression *"passer la nuit blanche,"* which means to pass the night without sleep.
2. *En* literally refers to relation or connection. Here it involves bringing disparate experiences into an intellectual or spiritual synthesis, a kind of comprehensive understanding. For further illumination of the idea, consult Chapter 32 in this book.

encounters. That individual self is like a leaf trembling in resonance with the sounds of the universe that permeate everything or else like a drop in an ocean wave affected by wind and tide.

In this great river of life that flows endlessly, there were moments of deep feeling when I realized that my life is a gift. Each such moment resembles an eternal spring gushing forth with the joy of "being helped to live and helping others to live." We can live as recipients of life from all[3] others and all else. Striving to live with all, I present this book as a kind of "landscape of encounters."[4] Even if it has the imperfect form of a fragment, it nevertheless is a portrayal of thoughts and experiences that call on privileged instants in the process, instants by which I have been coming to encounter myself.

So in this little book where I set out to convey a single idea to my Japanese readers, I now share that same, more varicolored thought with readers of English. My idea first permeated a collection of essays published serially in the Japanese-language magazine *Reirō*. What I emphasized there was the truism that Japan is in the world and the Japanese people are members of the human species. This seemingly simple fact is, in my country, obscured by an ingrained undertow of feeling that sharply separates "Japan" from "world" and "inside" from "outside."[5] To live in a country with Japan's clear-cut boundaries is to risk being condemned to a kind of mental isolation even if it is sometimes "happy isolation" – the destiny of an island country.

However, cultural diversity is indeed a treasure for humanity, and we must realize that it is a necessary condition for a fully human existence. Even though we may sometimes feel that the differences among the many cultures approach incompatibility, whenever we go deep enough we discover that they are all linked as one and therefore form a fundamental and complex unity.

Whenever any country or civilization realizes the deep connectedness of all human beings, it will be able to send a positive message for the rest of us and for future of humanity.

---

3. *Subete* means "all" in the sense of all that is really the universe. What follows shows that Hattori attains the insight that ultimately includes what is *in* you, me, and him as well as what is "outside" of us.
4. *Deai no fūkei* may be translated either as "landscape of encounters," as here, or "scenes of encounter."
5. To persons outside insular Japan it may come as a surprise to learn that the Japanese have engaged in long searches for their "uniqueness." Too often these inquiries have taken nasty turns toward separatism or nationalism. But ethnocentrism is universally difficult to avoid. Too much emphasis on what is "mine" may cause any lover of one's own self, country, or religion to esteem it so highly that it is above criticism or correction. Hattori has written me, "As for Americans, it is only when they realize that American culture is not the only culture that they can send a right message to the world." Compare this with his last line in this preface.

Acknowledgements
By Wallace Gray

My chief acknowledgement sums up all the rest: Deepest gratitude for
All I've met, All that flows and grows, dies and rises. . . .

The All is so great because the tiniest glint within it is an angel of light. Here I allude to my "glinters," who are not tiny in their helpfulness. Like light itself, which remains a mystery, they shine wondrously. Thanks, thanks, thanks, by categories:

Institutions. In particular I wish to give sincere thanks to the Institute of Moralogy in Japan for their contribution that has made this book possible. We are also deeply appreciative of the time and talent provided by University Press of America in the person of Samantha Kirk, Acquisitions Editor. She and each UPA associate who had a hand in getting us into print and on the market deserve a lot of credit for their courtesy, promptitude and perspicacity in untangling the jams I worked myself into. Asian Research Services' Nelson Leung, as publisher of *Asian Profile* and numerous related monographs, has had long experience with me and my difficulties. He has now, as Grandmother Gray used to say, "risen to the occasion" by leading the ARS team through the camera-ready copy for our book. Also, in the publishing line are *The Winfield Daily Courier* and *The Wichita Eagle* whose editors we thank for graciously permitting us to cite their articles. Finally, I wouldn't even have had the "lift" to become engaged with the foregoing institutions were it not for Southwestern College with which I have been intimately associated for more than half a century. In terms of research guidance and administrative support I remember especially Academic Dean Andy Sheppard and librarians Beth Sheppard, Veronica McAsey, Robert Perret, and Cheryl Barnett.

Individuals from 2nd graders to professional artists, historians; graduate and undergraduate students, football players (amateur and aspiring), food servers and chefs; ministers and confused folks – all those nameless ones whose conversations, critiques and responses to an emerging manuscript, or to our moment-to-moment steering of this project, helped build a book. Among our college's teaching staff, biologist Pat Ross and historian Steve Woodburn gave exemplary advice and interchange. Mentee Davion Mitchell provided me with a human sounding board and youthful voice in our intergenerational enterprise.

Family and Friends. Beloved wife Ina for patience with me in the on-and-on task of revising, rereading, consulting, and updating in such a rapidly changing world; her counsel frequently filled the void in my own business acumen and finesse. I treasure daughters Toni and Tara for being who they are, that is, persons accomplished in their careers and daughterly advice! To scholar-ministers Dale Robison I send thanks for supportive comments and quotable quotes.

Nick Warner helped clean up most of my solecisms; Nick has the aptitude for turning drudgery into a game. We cleared up many clause and comma inconsistencies, with the result that just before Christmas he exclaimed, "So many different types of clauses to consider this December: restrictive, independent, subordinate, and SANTA!" and, to avoid going into a "comma-coma," he promised, "I'll also try to avoid asking for too many commas for Christmas."

Further accolades go to Dr. Sidney Brown, longtime friend and encourager in Japanese studies; Keith Chuvala, Hebraist and NASA computer guru, for providing his warm and versatile assistance. Along the same line, I proclaim that without Southwestern College's Steve Ruggles and his all-day-every-day availability to everybody, I would by now have shattered into ashes of indecision over whether to cuss Information Technology or praise it. Individuals such as he assist us all to appreciate the cornucopia of benefits IT provides.

Eiji Hattori and the Firefly
Wallace Gray's Introduction

This book shines intermittent sparks beyond all the more glaring lights of megalopolises. It is a translation of Eiji Hattori's *Deai no Fūkei – Sekai no Naka no Nihon Bunka* (Reitaku Press, 1999). Literally, the title means, "Scenes of Encounter – Japanese culture in a global context." The author and I have decided to translate and rewrite the original in order to update and enhance the message without distorting the beauty and power of its "scenes of encounter." Most footnotes and text boxes, as well as all references to fireflies are mine. In addition to these editorial functions, I have worked as principal translator, with important assistance from Eiji Hattori and others.

Lest one facet of Hattori's life and career escape the reader, I want to emphasize his dedication to face-to-face dialogue. The president of Tokyo University credited Professor Hattori with designing the 2007 Tokyo UNESCO conference on "New Stakes for Cultural Diversity." He gave this credit at a conference in Madrid on "Dialogue on All Religions." Hattori sees the tremendous importance of the latter conference because it was organized by King Adbullah of Saudi Arabia and the Muslim World League, attracting perhaps 1000 participants including King Carlos.

* * *

Several unusual integrators join this enterprise. For the sake of maximum understanding, excuse my familiarity in addressing a short letter to you. Let's suppose you've written me a query about how to use this book to become a "truly global learner." Here's a partial answer:

Dear Inquirer,

First be attentive to hints in the text about the "Mystery of the 21st Century," also to our suggestions for addressing the problem implicit in the mystery. Whatever it is, it is NOT, at bottom, "the clash of civilizations." Three words describe what kind of clash is involved, namely, the "clash of ignorance," but the whole book needs perusal for our case to be fully rounded out.

Please try to view each of the encounters in this book as a winding trail, not a superhighway. Such paths are illumined from time to time by the gentle winking of lightening bugs. Sometimes the end of the trail may be important enough for you to become breathless as you climb toward it. However, the mysteriously illuminative sparks emitted along every inch of the path are important in themselves.

MORAL: No matter how steep or gentle the climb, never get so out of breath you forget to *breathe* the *beauty*, even should your nose lead you briefly off the main trail of our book.

— Initialed by a reformed moralist, wg
(coauthor, translator, editor)

The Firefly

What I know about fireflies is strongly conditioned by the kid-ignorance of one who encountered them as fun creatures to chase, and as luck allowed, to capture in fruit jars. Obvious even to a child is their ability, when bunched in a jar, to shed quite a bit of light....

I didn't grow up to be a biologist, so don't expect too much of me as I give you a quick and dirty layman's account of these little wonders:

Life cycle. Pretty short. My ball-park guess = 2 months, maybe two or three weeks for the adult male.

Sex life. Short and hungry. No food or very little. As I recall, the adult phase is only for procreation, no eating. Sounds like fun – or does it!?

Communication Skills. Kind of a Morse code between the sexes about who pairs with whom, and perhaps about dangers from predators.

Energy efficiency. The firefly has figured out a way to create light with practically no waste in the form of heat. Pretty cool, eh? (Scientists think so.)

The cultivation of the aesthetic sense is an oft neglected but most helpful way to deal with strange and hazardous matters. The poetic and prophetic flashes from Eiji Hattori's leadership as principal author do point to better ways and better days.

* * *

This Firefly Hunt has been given wings! One might even say that this book is becoming a kind of aerial Pilgrim's Progress. To view fireflies in unfamiliar terrain requires something besides the fireflies themselves. Without a guide, the tiny "flying lights" might lead a non-flier right off a cliff! Consider Hattori our main guide and me his anxious assistant.

At the end each of the book's chapters in its first edition there was a one-page enhancement. It helped Japanese readers more fully appreciate the "tea for two" that the author had served them. In those endnotes Hattori was able to presuppose familiarity with Japanese history and culture. One of the things we undertook in this book was to transform those notes to bring out their universal significance while restating their ideas and information in ways perhaps more accessible to readers of English. While these are co-authored Bridges, Hattori has put me in charge of them. Words I've elected to use from Hattori's notes to Japanese readers are either placed in italics, quotes or indented block form. Each Bridge (as is true of the book as a whole) is intended to aid anyone who wishes to use compassionate wisdom to deal more creatively with individuals, ideas or cultures at wide variance from what is familiar. Text boxes allow me to further engage the reader with our Mysterious Progress through Strangeness.

As I worked in our college library's reference room, a student librarian visited with me from time to time. These interruptions proved a priceless stimulus for the re-shaping of this book. It came about this way. The student, Mr. Davion Mitchell, was re-shelving items one day when he lingered perilously long over one page in the philosophy book he was handling. Somewhat to the surprise of both of us, this resulted in his asking me to mentor him in moral and philosophical thinking. You'll hear more from him as we go along.

We often pondered the meaning, if any, of the general or abstract terms all of us keep running across. An example would be the phrase, "truly global learner" on the title page of this book. Such phrases often cause us to ask ourselves, "What's that?" or, as here,

WHO?!

With gentle, inviting tones, I would like to try to beguile myself, Davion, and any bewildered reader with this answer:

Whoever encounters – truly encounters a firefly or two – or,
more prosaically – a
global prophet, a horrific or soothing event, a Zen master; a UNESCO news item; or, the Way of Tea, a Black Sky, caring saint (secular or religious), a real-live existentialist; or, a far-out dream, elegant lady, moment of beauty in cosmos or creature; or, an instance of war, terrorism, or peace; or, with deference to Eiji Hattori, his
"Genuine introduction to Japanese culture," and . . .

Whoever does not run away
promises
to be or become
One Truly Global Learner.

Breathless from this outburst, I'll now pause to write out my acknowledgments. You will find them immediately following the "Author's Preface" above; Hattori's are eloquently set forth in our book's "encounters."

Part I
Deep Encounters

Light Metaphor

To get the full metaphoric potential of the firefly's gentle light, one must discover the traditional Japanese firefly hunt.

As a turning point amidst natural and family catastrophes including bankruptcy, a lowly firefly appears as a harbinger of hope in Tanizaki's novel *The Makioka Sisters*, Book Three, Chapter 4.

Expect sparks of firefly illumination to fall on some of the encounters delineated in what follows.

1

Buddhas of Chartres
A Deep Encounter

When Professor Keiji Nishitani first saw the statues of saints standing in a row in Chartres Cathedral, he said, "They are just like Buddhas, aren't they?"

In 1961 I made a thirty-three-day sea voyage from Japan. That year I was to continue doctoral studies at the Sorbonne as a student from abroad on a French government scholarship.

It was a wonderful trip. We set out toward the end of August in a white French passenger ship named Vietnam that called at ports in seven countries; we finally disembarked at Marseilles. I would eventually make hundreds of trips by air here and there in the world, but after a lapse of more than 40 years, what I most remember is that voyage.

The ocean changed its lights and colors morning and evening, and once for three days all one could see was ocean, with not even the shadow of an island appearing. Then I felt the immensity of the earth, as well as its variety of climates and cultures. Each of the cities we visited cherished a civilization grown in its own unique "climate." As we moved from East to West, each city presented a different face.

When you travel at a leisurely ship-paced rate, as I did, you may at times be moving toward cultures strikingly different from all you have previously experienced. Each port of call will perhaps have surprises not met in previous layovers. Then one will appreciate the time between ports as a chance to digest each new experience and fix it in one's memory.

In one of his books the Japanese philosopher Arimasa Mori once told of his arrival in Marseilles. It was very similar to what my generation of Japanese students experienced except for the way he recalled it, "When I was standing there looking up at the Basilica of Notre Dame de la Garde on the hilltop, I felt that there must be something hard, rigid, resistant in Paris where I was bound, something that would reject me. I almost wanted to return home on the same ship."

In contrast, my generation of students passed smoothly through Marseilles without such a feeling of constraint. Paris has been much admired as the city for young men majoring in literature or philosophy. From the 13th century many and varied students have lived in *Quartier Latin* where the Sorbonne is situated. Artists have been drawn to Montparnasse and Montmartre. The Latin Quarter was the old center of Paris in the Middle Ages and has continued to be a students' town. It is on the Left Bank of the Seine. (When one faces downstream to the west or southwest, the bank on the left is naturally the Left Bank.) Montparnasse and Montmartre are famous as magnets for artists living in the 19th and 20th centuries; Saint-Germain-des-Prés is remembered as a gathering place for Existentialists in the mid-20th century.

The backstreets and narrow lanes are permeated by the smells and scents of life from many centuries. For me there was the enjoyment of the chestnuts[1] falling around me with sudden little knock-knock sounds as I walked along the Champs-Élysées while autumn was in full swing.

The school term at the Sorbonne begins late. Finally, at the end of October when students thronged into an old-fashioned building, I joined the lineup. An official doorkeeper was holding the auditorium door open for us. In accordance with custom, he wore a big chain around his neck from which was suspended a conspicuous key.[2]

In order to see as much as possible and to make as many friends as possible, I joined all kinds of student tours. My excursions began from the Parisian suburbs and extended to England and even Greece. The first year far exceeded any dreams I might have had before going to Europe.

When my beloved professor Keiji Nishitani of Kyoto University[3] informed me that he was planning to pay a visit to Paris, it had been a long time since we had seen each other. What immediately came to mind when I received the happy

---

1. For the biologically interested, the "chestnuts" that Hattori heard dropping as he walked along the Champs-Élysées are "horse chestnuts," *marron* in French; their tree belongs to the family *Aesculus hippocastanum* and is related to the American buckeye.
2. The "doorkeeper" mentioned in the text of the chapter is further explained by Hattori himself: "In French, *huissier* ("doorkeeper") might be rendered 'usher' or, perhaps, 'bailiff'. This person actually guards the door. His key was still used at the time I was a student at the Sorbonne in 1961."

news of his coming was that I would love to take him to see Chartres Cathedral.

About a hundred kilometers southwest of Paris, we entered a gently undulating plain in the ancient province of Beauce. Shortly thereafter the silhouette of Chartres Cathedral with its two bell towers capped by their steeples appeared to float up before our eyes from behind the obscuring rise in the plain. This is a scene expertly sketched in Marcel Proust's *Remembrance of Things Past*.

The cathedral was built during the high Middle Ages in Europe and occupies land considered holy by Druids before the advent of Christianity. Chartres was completed in no more than forty years, a wonderfully short time for cathedral construction of that period. Believers said, "It is for Black Mary who had no house of her own." Those who had money gave money. Physically strong men offered their labor, and carpenters dedicated their skills. Men and women, haves and have-nots, together made up the number of those who each helped make the cathedral a reality. That is why Chartres is an even more beautiful cathedral than others that are grander or that required more money or time to complete.

> **The Thought-Firefly**
>
> Like the first firefly of the season, a thought may appear out of nowhere. On other occasions the stage seems pre-arranged for the first wee winkings in one's backyard or on a walk. Hattori's trip with his esteemed teacher to Chartres prepared him for the appearance of a lovely thought-firefly. It surprised and enlightened both individuals.

In the construction of this cathedral there emerged a mysterious harmony reflecting a fusion of the Romanesque and Gothic styles. From this harmony we who are visitors to the cathedral receive an invitation into the world of devout prayer and meditation. This invitation is embodied in the sounds flowing from the pipe organ and in the beams of light streaming in through the stained glass windows – especially from their blue tones, known as Chartres blue.

At the front entrance, the façade consists of a statue of Christ surrounded by a number of saints (Jesus' disciples) standing in a row. Romanesque sculpture bequeathed simplicity to posterity.

It was while standing there gazing at that ensemble of statuary that Professor Nishitani uttered the words: "They are just like Buddhas, aren't they?"[4] In that

---

3. Keiji Nishitani was the most distinguished disciple of Kitarō Nishida, a major Japanese philosopher of the Kyoto University tradition. As a synthesizer of Japanese Zen Buddhism and other Japanese philosophic traditions with Western philosophy, Nishida is often likened to the process philosopher Alfred North Whitehead.
4. When Nishitani speaks of "Buddhas," the reader should understand that the word "Buddha" can refer not only to the historic Buddha, Gautama, but to various manifestations or successors called *bodhisattvas*.

one comment, I experienced a feeling of scales falling from my eyes. And then I woke up with a thought: *Even if cultures belong to different currents, they may encounter each other at the deeper levels.*

Before that moment of insight, whenever I had viewed a Buddhist statue in different countries, a sense of incongruity had lingered. You see, in my younger days I tended always to make a rigid distinction between Buddhism and Christianity. Then I could never have entertained a thought such as Nishitani expressed on that occasion. However, the comment issued quite naturally from the mouth of this leading figure of religious philosophy.

If we think about it, the human civilization born in the central part of southern Eurasia began to develop and evolve while changing form and spreading East and West during a period of several thousand years.[5] At almost the same time on both the eastern and western ends of Eurasia, there appeared a beauty that reflects a deepening of human spirituality. Herein lies a great hope: in humanity's core we may discover the possibility of living together in the future.

Bridge 1

The author characterizes the trip with which he begins this first encounter as the most memorable among hundreds made over a forty year period. Perhaps this early trip was the seed that flowered in the later Maritime Silk Road voyage in the Fulk-al-Salamah (Ark of Peace). This project was Eiji Hattori's brainchild and is described in his *Letters from the Silk Roads* (New York: University Press of America, 2000). We might even use the overworked term "culture shock" to characterize the encounter from which much of his creativity flowed.

Davion Mitchell, the 22-year-old student athlete I'm tutoring in philosophy, would like to ask a question.

"Yes, Dr. Gray, how would you define culture shock?"

"Let's assume for now it has the most to do with cultural geography. As I see this first chapter, culture shock is plainly visible in philosopher Mori's first contact with France and in Professor Hattori's encounter with some of the representations of the Buddha outside of Japan. These are cultural and intellectual expressions of the phenomenon. In contrast to religious and philosophical culture shock, I think also of gross culture shock. Once, my wife served corn on the cob to us while a Japanese student was living with us.

---

5. *Western saint statuary in the 12th and 13th centuries was the product of a time when there was a deepening of the Western spirit in accordance with the Christian tradition. It corresponded to what was happening in the Kamakura Era (1185-1333), which reflected a deepening spirituality in Japanese Buddhism. The spiritual intensification that occurred in those identical periods manifested itself in the kinship of sculpture seen in the two culture areas at the opposite ends of Eurasia.* – EH

Davion interrupted with, "I love corn on the cob!"

"So do most Americans, but when we lifted the cobs to our mouths and began in good Midwest fashion to chew off the kernels, rotating the cob as we stripped it, our student exclaimed, 'Ugh. How barbaric!' I believe she was experiencing culture shock in its most primitive, gut-reaction form. A missionary friend, who served effectively in the Philippines for many years, used to tell audiences, 'The last thing to be converted is the stomach.'"

* * *

Professor Hattori has explained his double doctorate. His description is an example of what I would call, "comparative academics." He was admitted to the Sorbonne on a French government scholarship to complete his doctorate begun at Kyoto University. He was considered by the French to already have a "University Doctorate," and his high ranking on the oral examination qualified him for "the State Doctorate course."

The French system at that time had two kinds or levels of doctor's degrees, the university and state levels. Hattori adds, "This system in France has now been changed into an international one, which is somewhat similar to the American doctorate system."

2

Water *Is* Life
Thinking with the Mediterranean poet Paul Valéry

Life emerged between 3.6 and 3.8 billion years ago from the ocean, as from a mother's womb. At that time, because of the encounter of water with light it underwent a metamorphosis into what we know as living organisms.

"When we look at a blade of grass or gaze at a big tree and then try to imagine what it is, it is like nothing so much as a great river streaming up through empty space" ("In Praise of Water"). These are the words of Paul Valéry, words that Yujirō Nakamura has recorded in his *Compendium of Human Knowledge*. In the first half of the 20th century, this extraordinary poet, who was born in Sète City, which faces the Mediterranean Sea, produced essays of penetrating intelligence. When Tatsuo Hori, a writer from northern Japan, wrote the book *Kazetachinu* (Wind Rises) describing something like life's ephemeral flame, he was thinking about the poem of Paul Valéry, "*Le Cimetière marin*" (The Graveyard by the Sea), where the poet states, "*Le vent se lève! . . . Il faut tenter de vivre!*" (Wind rises, try to live!) In Hori's book his use of the poem refers to the fleetingness of life.

The poet could see the Mediterranean from the his window. He arose at five daily, entered the sea, and swam until the morning sun dyed the water's surface. Then when he returned to his room he ground some aromatic coffee for himself. After finishing two savory cups, he engaged in his daily routine of writing until noon. In the afternoons he never wrote another word.

In the aforementioned literary fragment, "In Praise of Water," he sees a tree's form as something that reminds him of "water facing the sky as it seeks the light." Water "produces an image of something that yearningly stretches through branches and leaves toward the sunlight." We can do no less than admire this keen insight. The entire history of life on this earth is hereby condensed into the image, "Water is life."

Life emerged 3.8 billion years ago in the sea as from a mother's womb. At that time, life as it emerged was not at all alien to the environment of water from which it emerged. Water itself metamorphosed into an organic form called life.

According to Haeckel's famous theorem, "Ontology recapitulates phylogeny," that is to say, the development of the individual repeats in a very short time the entire development of the species, indeed of life in general.[1] In their evolution, all organisms have migrated from the womb of the sea to land. The human embryo experiences the same kind of change in its transition from its mother's womb to the outside world of land and air. Our blood is formed of the very same ingredients as seawater.

If one thinks about it, 70% of the body is water, and most trees and plants are 90% water. The disappearance of water means the extinction of life. Whenever people roam in the red-hot desert sands they may go without food, beer or *sake*, but they seek one thing, water. While Tetsurō Watsuji was comparing cultures of the desert zones in his work "Climate" he aptly referred to the damp and warm monsoon winds that blow in Southeast Asia as "winds of life."[2]

Should the rainy season be gloomy and depressing for us? It surely seems so. However, for a farmer, it provides the water of life. We Japanese surely must not forget to have a sense of gratitude for the plentiful blessings of nature. Its greenness springs from soil touched by an abundance of sun and water. Even in our Japanese textbooks we see the statement, "Japan is a country with no natural resources." I have a feeling that, when I am reading them, I am reading a textbook in 19th-century industrialized Europe where the fossil fuels of coal and oil, as well as such raw materials as iron and copper, were considered essential for the progress of industry and nation.

Let's present an anecdote for those who really think that Japan has no resources.

The time was just after the first oil shock of 1973. A delegation from an emirate of the Arabian peninsula turned up in Japan. They were at our welcoming party. A Japanese cabinet minister said to an Arabian sheik, "I envy you because your country has oil" – to which the sheik replied instantly, "If it were possible to

---

1. In other words, evolution in its exceedingly long unfolding has left a trace of its story in the development of the individual embryo. This is evidenced in various ways, for example, in the gill cleft found in a certain phase of the human embryo's transformation.
2. The book's title "*Fudō*" means "climate" or "physical features," or even "environment" or "biosphere."

exchange my country's oil for your country's water, I would do so immediately."

Doesn't this retort give wonderful expression to the fact that, as a natural resource, Japan's water is even more precious than the oil of Arabia? Here's another keenly interesting example.

Several years ago an experiment called "Biosphere 2" was performed in the middle of the Arizona desert. By means of an autonomic device that regulated the air and water, eight men and women were supposed to live in a huge dome for two years completely cut off from the external world. It was a reproduction of a miniature earth including its rivers and lakes, its tropical and temperate forests, and its farmlands with their barns and sheds for livestock and other domestic animals. Thousands of species of flora and fauna were brought in. Underground, in a large computerized room, a regulatory system imitating nature adjusted conditions so that life could survive even on Mars. However, in a year the experiment broke down because the water became degraded, so the experimenters had to introduce both fresh water and air.

The value of the trillion-dollar experiment will be proved if it stimulates a "conversion of our thinking." Then we shall realize that whether we are poor or rich, merely living on the earth from Mother Nature's yearly bounty is a blessing worth more than a trillion dollars.

When you visit Southern France, you'll sooner or later come across that fiery cypress tree that the artist van Gogh has painted. Van Gogh captured the light for which the southern France is noted. The "Graveyard by the Sea" where Paul Valéry once slept is a hill overlooking the southern city of Sète. From that point the Mediterranean stretched out limitlessly. Under a sun showering light, I saw a glittering sea overflowing with Renaissance blue.[3]

Bridge 2

The life and work of Paul Valéry (1871-1945) are briefly characterized in the Microsoft Encarta 98 Encyclopedia. He "is considered one of the greatest of modern philosophical writers in verse and prose." Encarta goes on to summarize his work as the presentation of "a conflict between contemplation and action that must be resolved artistically in order to grasp the meaning of life."

The context for the line "The wind rises, I have to try to live" is the contrast between the stillness of the cemetery and the flow and surge of the sea. In human terms it evokes the contrast between the sometimes too static meditation of the philosopher and the dynamism of the only important thing that remains for us to

---

3. This dark yet somehow transparent blue was the theme-color of the Italian Renaissance. Note Hattori's circular style, moving from the esthetic to the ecological and back again to the esthetic. Some readers may sense the form of a rising *spiral* rather than a circle.

fall back on – action. The colorful, lively sail of a boat tossed by wind and wave evokes joyful feelings and thoughts in sharp contrast to the gloomy meditations of a thinker suddenly snatched from his dreams of the absolute.

Hattori's note to Japanese readers gives a comparative view in global perspective:

> One third of Eurasia is a desert zone. I gained a vivid impression of that fact when I flew from Islamabad across the Karakoram mountain range to Beijing. When one crosses the Karakoram Range by jet, then the Taklamakan Desert, the Gobi Desert, and so on, all continue to turn reddish under one's very eyes for five long hours. As I gazed down at all this, I realized how vast the deserts are.
>
> As anyone approaches Japan by plane, they must realize that the archipelago is green. Where there is greenness there is wealth; water in abundance is wealth. However, we Japanese have gotten used to the blessings of nature and, baby-like, simply depend on this kindness.
>
> Europe domesticated nature, and became accustomed to taking care of nature. That care alone shows that nature is treated seriously. Similarly, for the people of Arabia water is the greatest treasure. Both jewels and expensive name-brand items take second place to water in value.

Lester R. Brown, the world-environmentalist who founded the highly respected Worldwatch Institute, in 2003 published *Plan B: Rescuing a Planet Under Stress and a Civilization in Trouble*. In this book, he tells us (as summarized by a reviewer), "Humanity crossed a threshold in 1980. For the first time our activities outpaced the planet's ability to regenerate."

The editors of *World Ark*, a Heifer International publication, devoted their Fall 2003 issue to "Troubled Waters." In addition to the review of the Brown book, the publication includes Sandra Postel's feature article on the issue's theme: "An increasing shortage of freshwater, the basis of life on land, looms, and the problems are outpacing the solutions." However, there are solutions – alternatives that Brown, Postel and many others are detailing.

3

To Be or To Appear[1]
Remembering Jean-Louis Barrault

"The puppets played like men, and the men, like gods!"

The puppets played like men, and the men, like gods! I heard this pronouncement in a resolute and resounding voice in the salon of the Odeon Theatre in the center of the Latin Quarter of Paris as it was being enveloped by smoky tear gas. It was sometime during May of 1968.

That was when student riots started from the Sorbonne and spread like fire all over the world. In France the workers joined in it, and it developed into the "May Revolution" that soon paralyzed the whole country. In that central Latin Quarter where the Odeon Theater is located, barricades were thrown up, and the smoke from the tear gas shells fired by the riot police became quite thick in the historic theater. At that very moment, a reception was taking place in the salon of the Odeon to celebrate the successful last performance of Bunraku Theater in Paris.

People were wondering anxiously, "Can we safely get out of France tomorrow?" The man who had sprung to his feet in the center of the salon, as if he intended to extinguish the audience's growing uneasiness concerning the atmosphere of revolution outside the theater, expressed more with his short

---

1. In Japanese the title means literally "to be *and* to appear," or perhaps, "being something as compared to appearing to be something."

utterance than a hundred reassuring compliments could have done. He put into concise words the essence of Japanese traditional puppet theater (*bunraku*). His attitude, his voice and short words – instead of a long speech – electrified the audience.

The speaker was Jean-Louis Barrault, who, for a long time prior to the May 5th Revolution, had presided over the palatial Odeon Theater – a "palace of nations." As both director and actor, he was often spoken of as one of the greatest figures in the twentieth-century theater world. The movie *Les Enfants du Paradis*,[2] "The Children of Paradise" (1945) introduced him to the world of the silver screen and suddenly made this young man a world-renowned star. However, after that he declined all offers from the film industry and devoted himself solely to the stage.

Why? I wish to answer that question with the words of Paul Claudel, Baurrault's favorite poet. "Theatre is the communion between the stage and the spectators."

There is a moment in which the stage and audience become one, when art is born as both parties commune with each other. According to the Japanese idiom, "It's a duel with real swords." One has the striking impression of an experience in which there occurs highly effective communication with the audience that does not depend exclusively on words. What is imagined here suggests invisible threads straining and stretching to link stage and spectators. I had this kind of experience even in high school where I engaged myself, along with Kunie Tanaka[3] and others, to create a theatrical circle.

My initial encounter with Jean-Louis Barrault was in 1960 when he first participated in the Osaka Festival as leader of the Renaud-Barrault Troupe (named after his wife Madeleine Renaud and himself). That occasion also gave him the opportunity to lecture in the Kyoto Franco-Japanese Institute, and it also gave me the chance to say to him in that assembly, "I know you love Noh theater, but do you think it is possible to fuse an art, like Noh, which internalizes everything, with your own art which exteriorizes everything?" Madeleine Renault, his lifetime companion, turned in her seat and beamed at me. Barrault himself also particularly liked this question, so it provided the chance for me to become the Kyoto guide for this famous troupe. Also, I was personally invited to their Osaka performance.

A year after that, when I began to study abroad in Paris, a complimentary ticket from Barrault was awaiting me at each opening performance at the Odeon Theater. It became my habit after performances to visit his dressing room backstage for a pleasant discussion. Also, it was here that I was introduced to the playwright

---

2. "Children of Paradise" here refers to persons holding seats near the ceiling. "Paradise" had the cheapest seats in the house.
3. Tanaka in time became a famous film star.

Eugène Ionesco.[4]

One day I discovered among the publications of the Odeon Theater an essay by Barrault himself. It's an explanation of humanity's real character and is entitled, "The Two Basic Desires of Human Beings." He states, "The first is *to be* (*être*) and the second, *to appear* (*paraître*)." Drama limits itself to putting heart and soul into "Appearance" as symbolized by a mask (persona).[5] In Luxemburg Park in front of the Odeon Theater there stands the statue of a young man wearing a mask.

At Barrault's invitation Hisao Kanze, the head of the Kanze school of Noh, came to Paris for a brief stay. Shortly after his arrival, I planned an "Evening of Noh." I did this as president of the residents' committee of the *Maison du Japon* in the University City Center.

My conception of the evening's order had two main components:

1. Two lectures on Noh, one by J. L. Barrault on his discovery of Noh, another by René Sieffert, who translated the main books of Zeami, founder of Noh.
2. One demonstration by Hisao Kanze, who had to dance alone without scenery or costume. (Such dancing is referred to as *sumai*, dance without costume).

That evening Barrault spoke these words:

> In the past when I went to see the first performance of Japanese Noh in Lyon, I did not understand it at all. But on the occasion of my Tokyo performance I was invited to Kanze's home as the only guest. At midnight in his Noh hall he performed a single dance. I was there and suddenly understood everything about Noh. That experience was something like heaven's enlightenment.

The next day I invited Kanze to a restaurant in Montparnasse. When I asked, "What is Noh looking for?" he gave me an unforgettable answer: "Noh seeks the beauty of *being there*." Whenever an individual has a full and fulfilled existence, that person sparkles as though crystallized into beauty itself. What Barrault was seeking does not differ from what Kanze was seeking. There is a type of personality that has slipped and fallen and yet continues to polish and perfect itself. Such a personality is an integral or integrated subjectivity. Its "appearing" is exactly its "existence." (It is what it seems to be.) It naturally emanates from its being in such a way that for it "to be" or "to appear" is one unitary act. On the

---

4. Eugène Ionesco (1909-1994), French dramatist born in Romania and famous for such plays as *The Bald Soprano* and *Rhinoceros*.
5. "Mask" and "persona" together are words intended to suggest the representation through voice and facial appearance of a character, as well as through a literal mask or costume.

contrary, the self that lacks subjectivity is buried in its group because it cares only about how it "appears."

When I returned to Japan I did not see Barrault again for at least three years.

Then sometime toward the end of 1972 I returned to Paris to take up my new post with UNESCO. On the first day of my return I providentially encountered him.

I had casually opened a newspaper when the headline jumped out at me: "BARRAULT AT ORSAY PROVISIONAL THEATRE TO PERFORM CLAUDEL." I set out immediately for the theater, and, once there, decided to wait in a nearby bistro till the theater opened. As soon as I pushed through the door of the bistro, I was amazed to see Barrault himself right before my eyes. He invited me to his table as though we were there together only yesterday!

When I expressed my worry that he looked a little haggard after having been driven away from the Odeon Theater by the May Revolution of 1968, he answered, "Freedom is something hard to live. However, now I am happy as a king."

Bridge 3

First, to review some of the most pertinent background information of this Encounter: Bunraku is a traditional and unique form of Japanese Puppet Theater deriving its name from Bunraku-za, a theater built by Bunraku-ken Oemurea who died in 1810.

Jean-Louis Barrault (1911-94) was a distinguished French actor, pantomimist, director, producer, and actor. He was director of the Odeon Theater in Paris, later renamed the Théâtre de France.

The intense feelings accompanying the May 5 Revolution may be inferred from the personal and professional consequences for Barrault in the aftermath. As a result of the support he gave the student-participants who seized one of the state-sponsored theaters, a dispute arose that caused him to resign from that theater, the Théâtre des Nations. With his wife he then returned to his original Renaud-Barrault Company. Zeami/Seami (1363-1443), who is also called Kanze Motokiyo, was an innovative dramatist and the inventor of Noh drama. He made a decisive turn from traditional Japanese theater, which was representational, toward more symbolic and Zen-influenced innovations. Like Greek drama, Noh Theater uses masks.

With these notes out of the way, we turn to the substance of Hattori's chapter. At the risk of a little repetition, the author and I are making explicit here what may simply be assumed by Hattori or else stated by him in a subtly artistic way.

In our correspondence, Hattori has succinctly described his concern for communion, which he and Barrault share. "For me communion is more than communication – it is to become *one*. This is my explanation of Barrault's refusal to continue to make films. The movie actor cannot experience this communion."

Then he significantly adds, "But the main theme of this chapter is to be and to appear. There are so many people who want only to appear."

Perhaps because he was what he appeared to be, Barrault was in voice and presence *like the gods*.

4

Being and Having
Learning from Gabriel Marcel

> Ordinarily, a person is convinced that the enhancement of one's existence depends upon the money, status, or possessions that one has. However, in reality, attachment to what one has wears away at one's existence.

In June of 1980, the people in UNESCO'S great meeting hall in Paris were excited in expectation of the arrival of the head of the Roman Catholic Church, John Paul II. Those waiting included representatives from all the member states with their different religions and UNESCO staffs. I understood that the primary reason for the pope's official visit to France was to issue a message to the world from this international body.

With the palm of my hand still warm from just having shaken hands with the pope while he mingled with those present, I inclined my ear to pay attention to the words of that white-robed man now on the stage. "According to Thomas Aquinas, 'We live a truly human life through *ars* (culture) and *ratio* (reason).' " On this basis, the Pope proceeded to open for us the core of his address.

> It is through culture that man as a human being becomes more human, "exists" more fully and has more "being." And it is therein that the fundamental distinction between what man is and what he has, between being and having, is grounded.[1]

When I heard these words, I sensed in them immediately the influence of the philosopher Gabriel Marcel, to whom I had dedicated the thesis for my Master of Arts. Nobody else has described so clearly the twin concepts of *being* and *having* that lie at the very heart of existence.²

He considered these to be quite distinct aspects of human existence; he went so far as to say that these two aspects are polar opposites of each other. The nub of one of Gabriel Marcel's astonishing remarks is that they are in inverse proportion to each other: "*Being* diminishes as *having* increases."

> Gabriel Marcel (1889-1973)
>
> Marcel is usually considered the first French Christian philosopher to become an exponent of existentialism. He was a contemporary of the more famous Jean-Paul Sartre, but his groundbreaking work immediately preceded and significantly differed from Sartre's.

Ordinarily, we are convinced that whoever has gained more money, status, or things exists at a higher level. However, the truth is that attachment to various kinds of possessions wears down the very existence of people so that these possessions even restrict that existence, resulting in the loss of true freedom. According to Marcel, people's real freedom consists in being available or receptive to others, in other words, being free to serve others at any time. The French term for this is *disponibilité* (disposability).

He says, "God, being all in all, has nothing (because God is perfect Being)."³ There are persons who have passed almost every bound in their efforts to draw close to God. Such persons are spoken of in the East as having "the Buddha nature." In Italy there was Saint Francis of Assisi and, in Japan, Ryōkan. Both are examples of people close to God. Such individuals are penniless by choice.

My thinking here recalls a far-away day when I was a student. During my early studies of French, I happened to wonder whether the verb *avoir* (to have) might contain the negative prefix "*a*" that is common to Indo-European languages. I realized that the prefix "*a*" means "not" and "*voir*" refers to seeing, so *a-voir* might mean non-seeing. This youthful interpretation suggests that "having" may be understood as "not seeing."

John Paul II was speaking in a way that reflected Marcel's terms but even more the pope's own conviction that culture is at the core of human existence. He is giving a hearty warning to the present age against getting dizzy struggling day and night "to have."

In my early twenties when I was fascinated by existentialism, I was worrying about how to overcome the solipsism that seems to be a necessary part of all

---

1. Here the translator uses the English wording supplied by E. Hattori based on his article published in *Reitaku Journal of Interdisciplinary Studies* (Vol. 5, No. 2, September, 1997, p. 7), "Towards a Transcultural Dialogue: the Role of UNESCO in the Development of Transdisciplinarity."
2. See Marcel's *Being and Having* (1935, Eng. trans., 1949).
3. In Japanese, the verb *dearu* can mean either "is" or "has."

existentialism. While wondering and wandering, I encountered Gabriel Marcel, the very person whose thinking could help me dispel my confusion. *Co-esse* (co-being or co-existence) is real existence. For Marcel the true understanding of existence lies not in "I" or "thou" but in "we"; that means that being-together takes priority over[4] individual existence.

Family and love occupy center stage in his understanding. Neither my own subjectivity nor the other's objectivity from my point of view can mean anything apart from what Marcel calls, "intersubjectivity." It is the subjectivity of "I and thou" in a relational context. Communion[5] or union/unity turns out to mean, "I and thou are mutual." If I am not to collapse into myself or else to be absorbed into the consciousness of the other, my "I" and your "thou" must be known and intersubjectively related in the Light of an eternal Thou (God). Marcel believed (as I now do) that without the eternal Thou, intersubjectivity is not possible. That is astonishing! As the light of the sun allows us to see one another, so the light of God allows us to experience correctly our relationship with one another. As far as I am concerned, to look at you and have insight into myself, there must be a thou (*toi* in French) and Thou (with the capital letter), in other words, the eternal Thou. I feel that this way of discovering God and grasping reality as co-being opens the horizon of hope for solitary and lonely individuals in the modern period.

It was Sartre who defined Gabriel Marcel as a Christian existentialist, but the gray-haired philosopher, whom I had the opportunity in Paris to know personally, did not like this kind of designation. I think that Marcel preferred the "follower of Socrates" as the appellation with which he was most comfortable. Until departing this world at eighty-four he philosophized daily with every breath he took, as Socrates did.

Deserving mention here is a report on a current topic of education. As a follow-up to the work of the Edgar Faure Commission of thirty or so years ago, UNESCO in 1997 convened an "International Commission on Education in the 21st Century." That commission published, "Recommendations and Guiding Principles in Education for Human Development." The recommendations rest on four pillars:

1. Learning to know
2. Learning to do
3. Learning to live together
4. Learning to be

---

4. *Saki* can also even mean that relational existence *precedes* individualized existence!
5. The word "communion" here means deep mutuality and interdependence. In the larger context of Marcel's philosophy, Communion (with the capital letter) can refer to the mystery of communion with God through Christ in what Roman Catholics call the Mass and Protestants, Communion.

A phrase that illuminates the fourth item in this list is "education of the whole person." In Japanese this is interpreted to mean "learning to live as a human being" or "philosophy for the sake of self-realization." However, it cannot be said that any of these is the perfect translation. I truly think that the meaning of "to be," when we meditate on the matter, is clarified by the words of Gabriel Marcel and those pronounced by the pope in connection with his official visit to France at the UNESCO meeting in 1980.

Bridge 4

With reference to the question of whether or when Marcel accepted the designation "existentialist" for himself, James Collins sheds a bit of light. He points out in the preface to *Being and Having* (Harper Torchbook edition, 1965), "In his latest writings, Marcel relents sufficiently to permit himself to be regarded as an existential thinker." However, Collins also points out that on occasion Marcel repudiated the name existentialist and, instead, called himself a "Christian Socratic." Chronology may not have been as important for Marcel as context and intention. When emphasizing his common ground with others of the school, he was an existentialist. When emphasizing his differences he was a Christian Socratic.

The somewhat difficult term "disposability" is further opened for us by Marcel's own words: "Charity [is] thought of as presence, as absolute disposability; I have never before seen its link with poverty so clearly. To possess is almost inevitably to be possessed. Things possessed get in the way." This edited quotation is from *Being and Having*, p. 69. The whole page is clear and important theologically, philosophically, and personally. English speakers refer ironically to "being owned by what we own." It's supposed to be the other way around. Most recently, we hear people saying, "The computer is supposed to serve us, but, more and more, *I'm serving it!*"

In explaining Marcel's thought to the Japanese, Hattori is suggesting to his fellow citizens that their increasingly materialistic culture is in danger of depriving them of a basic liberty – freedom from things. Now, as Hattori's work is gaining wider accessibility through translation, it recalls and reemphasizes Marcel's warning for a much larger audience.

Davion: Professor Hattori, could you please shed a bit more light on him as a person?"
H: My pleasure, Davion. Gabriel Marcel received Jewish blood from his maternal grandmother. Because of that and in spite of having a strict Catholic father, he was not baptized as an infant. However, he became a friend of the Boegner family, which was the spiritual pillar of Protestantism in Southern France, and he married a Boegner daughter, Jacqueline.

Once when my wife, Coline, and I were invited for supper at the Marcel residence, Marcel learned that my wife's family was on good terms with Mrs. Marcel's family. Since then the Marcels have shared an intimate feeling of friendship with our family.

Even as a thinker, Marcel was a person who stuck close to life's everyday events. Doing philosophy was like breathing for him. He refused to build "systems" but put heart and soul into the "reflections" he wrote in the tradition of French philosophy. However, we find at the core of his work the excellent concept of "mystery," which stands in contrast to scientific objects and pure objectivity.

Davion: Thank you. Marcel's close affinity for life and its mystery appeals to me. Also, my own immediate genetic inheritance is mixed. Mother is Black Baptist and father, Hispanic Catholic!

5
The Logic of the City
kō ("official") and *kōkyō* ("public")

The European city had an excellent system of self-defense, and for that reason, people in Europe gave distinct priority to a public approach to problems as opposed to a merely personal or private one. Citizens, in exchange for the protection of being allowed to live inside the castle walls of a city, came to see it as their obligation to show respect for the public well-being.

In the same Japan that is supposed to have become a postwar democracy, why are the words *kan* (official) and *min* (people) still used? These words, which even a speaker of Japanese might associate only with such English words as "government" and "citizen" respectively, actually have very feudalistic, even imperialistic overtones stemming from Japan's history. Imagine if Americans or other speakers of English were to go around speaking of "lords" and "subjects" instead of government workers and citizens. This gives the flavor of the problem we are considering here. Even the Japanese media use this kind of loaded language casually, unconsciously. In the streets one even hears the word *okami* (an old word for the emperor that quite literally means "the high one" or "highness"). Isn't this a wonder? In historical Japan, "cities" in the full meaning of the term have never existed. (Citizens in the West, of course, use the word "government" and have no equivalent word for "*okami*" in reference to their presidents or ministries.)

In historical Japan cities in the full meaning of the term have never existed. If we pay attention to this point, we will recognize that the Japanese notion of *kō* matches the English usage of "official" while the idea of *kōkyō* ("public") is as yet immature and undeveloped.

The word "city" in Greek is *polis* and in Latin *civitas*, from which French derives *cité* and English, "city." This originally referred to a city-state surrounded by a wall. Even now in certain cities a key is presented to any person elected as an honorable citizen, and that key will open the city's gate, which much earlier was the castle gate.

Traditionally, the Western city was an excellent "system of self-defense." In such a place, public interests clearly prevail over personal or private ones.[1] Citizens are the people who give attention to public affairs in exchange for the protection offered by the city when they are allowed to live inside it. There it made an important difference whether you were a citizen or not. For example, when a city is building a public place for a market, or a road on which to move troops swiftly, the work is a public enterprise, and the citizens who reside there must move when public interest dictates. If you are a citizen, you cannot at such a moment protect your own private rights. In contrast, persons living outside the walls simultaneously retain both freedom and its dangers.

Times change, and now cities no longer have the primary defense function.[2] This responsibility is sensed to have passed elsewhere. The reason is that modern cities are offering citizens such things as welfare, education, transportation, economic benefits, and means of communication. In exchange for receiving this kind of guarantee, citizens give priority to public or common interests over private rights. For example, when a certain district of Paris was being reorganized and reconstructed, a letter was sent out that said, "Please be prepared to leave your house a year from now. The city will provide you with a comparable residence in some other area. If it does not suit you, you may choose to receive equivalent indemnity." The uproar that would occur in Japan did not arise from either the letter or the action of the municipal government of Paris. The kind of uproar that occurred in connection with building the Narita International Airport on peasant land in the Tokyo area did not arise in Paris. When I returned to Tokyo some thirty years ago, it was amusing to see the arrangement of peasant houses. Some could be seen on either side of the new road, but one resisting house stood squarely where the new public highway was originally supposed to pass. The road simply branched around this symbol of defiance!

How did such a contrast in public awareness come about? The crazy-quilt arrangement of rows of houses in Tokyo demonstrates the difference of consciousness between the West and Japan, which made the famous architect Kenzō Tange lament, "Here city planning is impossible." We can admit that there

---

1. The Chinese character here used for "private" (私) suggests ego-centered, since it is usually pronounced *watakushi* meaning "I" or "me."
2. After 9-11-01, New Yorkers must certainly hope their city government is helping the federal government with the security of their city!

is the problem of the right to enjoy sunshine. But it is a rural or peasant[3] idea to say, "What's wrong with my building whatever I like on my land? It's none of your business." This is not the thinking of a citizen. The village idea is still evident in place names within the city of Tokyo. In Western Europe, city streets have names, but in Tokyo the streets lack proper names. In Tokyo, spaces have names but not the streets or avenues. If you see an avenue name, such as Aoyama-dōri, it is a nickname. In a farm village Taro-san (Mr. Smith or Jones in English) has a rice paddy. The most important fact about the paddy is that it belongs to a certain individual in his village. There is no name for the farm road or footpath between paddies. In contrast, since Kyoto was built as the capital, it had street names instead of these area names.

However, even Kyoto was an oriental capital, not a Western city. Even though this Japanese capital was an imitation of the Chinese city of Ch'ang-an (modern Xian), it is still not a city in either the Western or the Chinese sense.[4] Kyoto had city planning like Ch'ang-an but did not have a city wall.

We can ask, "Do the walls of castles that were built in the Azuchi-Momoyama Period (1568-1615) correspond to the Western system of group defense?" The answer is, "No, they do not." Beyond the moats of these castles were splendid encircling walls, but these castles were not a city.

There were groups of samurai who lived in the protected area between the inner and outer castle moats. In Europe many people who should have been citizens or bourgeois lived outside the castle walls. They lived in what the French call the *faubourg*. Originally meaning fort area, the word "*faubourg*" came to mean suburb, the outlying area around a city. The residents were "persons who live outside the castle walls."

At that time, in Europe and America the sense of citizenship that had formerly belonged to people living in city states such as Athens, passed into the consciousness of peoples living in modern nation states. Nationals (more or less literally connoting the people of a country) have become what are known in Europe and the Americas as "citizens." Moreover, the concept of modern citizenship has taken root in recent times. In the time of the French Revolution, the "Declaration of Human Rights" – more precisely, the "Declaration of the Human Rights of Citizens" – saw the light of day. Nevertheless even at the time of the Meiji Restoration in (1868) nothing changed regarding the understanding of citizenship in Japan. It was only a shifting of power from one feudal group to another.[5]

---

3. *Nōmin* can mean "farmer" or "peasant." Because Japan is closer to its feudalistic periods than many places in the West are to theirs, the denotations of "farmer" and "peasant" are still quite closely associated. The anecdote should not be allowed to color the emotive connotation for either all "farmers" or all "peasants."
4. In Japanese, "capital" is *kyō* (as in *Kyo*to, or its early names Heijō*kyō* and Heian*kyō*).

The distinction between functions or levels of human beings that began with the placement of the walls has been inherited intact. This uniquely Japanese castle tradition – one that depended on who had been inside and who outside the castle wall – is the source of the very distinction that still lies in the depths of Japanese consciousness.

We can see examples of this consciousness in the language. The inside of the castle walls is *kō* "official" while outside is *shi* "private." To vary the wording a bit, inside were *kan*, the "officials," while *min*, "the people," lived outside. Outside the walls live the inferior subjects, *shimojimo* (low people), who look up to the superior rulers, the *okami* (high people).[6] Even when the castle in Japan gave way to other centers of power and other names, such as the notorious *kasumigaseki*,[7] the feudal way of thinking of government still continued to persist. Now, a politician who is supposed to represent residents outside the "wall," once elected, acts as though he is a superior "insider."

Democracy arose in the city of Athens before the fifth century B.C. The agora where Socrates held discussions was a public plaza. There the citizenry gathered.

In our day, if Japan truly wants democracy, it must begin by ceasing to call public servants "the Court" (*kan*)[8] just because they live and work in the government sector. They should be civil *servants*, in other words, servants of other citizens. Also, politicians must not become trapped in the *kan*. Ironically, the challenging task facing democratic politicians is to cultivate a sense for citizenship in a country with no history of "citizen" as the concept has developed in the West. If leaders fail to do this, Japan may never become a fully civilized country. By

---

5. To understand this, some historical background is necessary. The shogun ruled for the emperor. In the 19th century certain daimyos (high lords) who were under the shogun wanted to replace the shogun and rule on behalf of the emperor themselves. The two most important daimyos at the time were the leaders of the Satsuma clan and the Chōshū clan, both from the western end of the Japanese archipelago. They and their retainers (lower samurai) displaced the shogun in the Meiji Restoration. This is often compared to the French and American Revolutions but was much more conservative politically. However, it brought great changes to Japan in the areas of education, military affairs, political reorganization, and the use of science, medicine, and technology.
6. This situation of power, prestige, and wealth reminds one of the old American joke about the highest stratum of society. "What is the upper crust?" "It's a few crumbs held together by a lot of dough." If the reader wonders whether Japanese peasants ever shared such jokes, Hattori agrees they did.
7. Foreign Office and all other ministries.
8. No English word properly translates *kan*, but "Court" (as in "royal or imperial court") conveys the sense that the government is *not* of the people, for the people, or by the people but something different from and above ordinary citizens.

the way, civilization means the way by which a citizen (πολίτης = *politēs*) shapes politics.[9]

Bridge 5

Hattori adds:

> Even in the Hanseatic League, which was neither a city nor a state, there was a kind of cooperation allowing citizens to consult. There were places and occasions for citizens to consult. We may easily see an inheritance in the West from the Greek tradition of collective wisdom based on consultation. . . . The ideal in the West has been that as long as you perform your duties as a citizen you have true liberty.

Such liberty, as we have seen, must be balanced by the common good in ways that allow the latter to restrict individual rights in order that social well-being not suffer.

Recall Hattori's anecdote above comparing a farmer's reaction in Japan with that of the Parisian city-dwellers involved in similar government regulation. For my part, I deplore the fact that many of my fellow Americans are forsaking some of their democratic roots. Middle class suburbs and the mansions of the superrich seem to be a self-confession of poor citizenship. Gross selfishness is too often reflected in the attempt to escape all the city's troubles – and the taxes to deal with them – while continuing to enjoy its many benefits.

I wonder whether Hattori, my very gentlemanly friend, is not thinking, "Better you say it than I!"

---

9. From πολτική is derived the word "politics" meaning the art or science of government.

6

The Light of Reason
Descartes and Noah's Ark

The most advanced present-day science is about to recommence dialogue with ancient human wisdom. However, what has opened such a perspective to science is the same light of reason found by Descartes in the 17th century.

The time period was that of the Thirty Years War (1618-1648). During the cold night of November 10, 1619, a young officer was sitting in a rocking chair before the fireplace alone in his room at an inn near the city of Ulm (or Olm) on the Danube.[1] He was lost in meditation.

Suddenly he was struck with an inspiration; it was the discovery of a "wonderful new basis for learning." This young man was René Descartes. According to what he wrote afterwards, his whole philosophical system came to him in that instant, with the details to be finished later.

The existence of the ego established by his discovery of the argument *cogito ergo sum* (I think, therefore I am) made Descartes famous as the father of modern philosophy. Even today "Cartesian logic" (that is, "the logic of clear proofs," or "the method of analytical geometry," as exemplified by Descartes) still exercises an overwhelming influence. It is my view that, somewhat apart from specific methodologies, his major discovery that night was his image of a Tree of Wisdom,

---

1. If you're curious about Descartes' "stove," consult Bridge 6.

the root of which was rational metaphysics; the trunk was natural science, and the branches were medicine, morality, and mechanics. So the basis of all this tremendous modern development was formed one night in an instant of grace.

Descartes' discovery at such a time and in such a way can rightly be regarded as a *pivotal experience*. If we rely on Arimasa Mori's expression to help us understand it, it was the kind of experience accompanied by "an acute, almost physical pleasure."

However, Descartes remained silent about it during a nine-year period until the publication of his first philosophical essay, *Rules for the Direction of the Mind*. One of his principal works, *Discourse on Method*, was only published in 1637 and another, *Meditations*, in 1642. Why the silence?

After his transformative discovery in that German camp in 1619, he went on soon thereafter to solve difficult mathematical problems and to write essays in natural science. His fame naturally rose, and it is rumored that the young man had already achieved a marvelous philosophical system at this time. Still he kept his silence.

What on earth was he doing for nine years? He was travelling. He wandered from place to place in various countries. We must consider the purpose of all this travel.

After he had doubted everything he reasonably could in 1619, he arrived at a universal truth of which he could say it alone could not be doubted. However, he thought once again he must attain certainty that this "truth" was not something based on traditions and customs of his own country, and that it was not a kind of self-satisfaction proceeding from ignorance of the customs or sense of values of people in other countries. The first principle on his list of *four principles of learning* was to avoid precipitate or prejudiced behavior. Descartes went abroad to use and test that principle by his own actions.

This same René Descartes, "the father of science in the 17th century," is also seen as a kind of initiator of our modern degradations of nature. In fact, I myself have mentioned his name in some essays in which I have criticized what I call "linear scientism."[2] However, what makes me wonder about some criticisms is that many people who have neither read Descartes nor studied his life still proceed in authoritative tones to criticize him. One must know his life to understand him.

Modern science, to which Descartes gave a tool in the 17th century, evolved in the 19th into an inflated estimation of what science is and can do. In short, it became a huge dogma called scientism. However, those who discovered the limits of "modern science" (now known as classic science) and who have identified

---

2. In its crudest form, scientism exalts the methods of science above all else. It splits fact and value, nature and spirit, thereby allowing the natural world to be desecrated by reductionistic analysis, exploitation, or destruction for the "progress" of knowledge and of "civilization."

its scientific failures are not theologians or philosophers but the scientists themselves. The most advanced science of today keeps making qualitative leaps or revolutionary turnabouts in its own course of development as science. What we see in this mutation is that humanity will again find possible a conversation between ancient wisdom and new discoveries. That night in Germany in his famous "room with a fireplace" Descartes opened a vista of hope illuminated by the "light of reason." Let us try to replace the word "reason" with "logos" (reasonable discourse or, more precisely and dynamically, "thinking discourse").

At the 1995 symposium commemorating the 50th anniversary of the founding of UNESCO held at United Nations University, the theme was "Science and Culture – a Common Path to the Future." In his keynote lecture, Kenzōburo Ōe quoted the German writer Mihael Ende, who used the Hebrew word pronounced *tewa* (also *tevah*):

> In Hebrew the word for boat is tewa and that word has an additional meaning in Hebrew. While it does mean boat or ark, it at the same time also signifies "verb."
> . . . .
> As for Noah, he was saved by the ark in the verbal sense, as though he was "arked."[3]

Also, Oe explained his idea about literature in this way:

> During periods when the world has been shaken by fury, the light of reason often shines. The American Declaration of Independence, the Declaration of Human Rights at the time of the French Revolution, and the Charter of UNESCO after World War II – all these are proof of the victory of Reason over Chaos. We must participate in worldwide discussions more and more, and train our reason for that. As global citizens we are completely members of Noah's family. Humanity is drifting – lost at sea. Will our dove return to us with a twig indicating that we once again are about to touch land? (Genesis 8:11)

Bridge 6

In connection with the importance of Descartes' deductive methodology, the author here uses the vivid verb *assuru* (oppress, overpower, overawe), which I

---

3. While the German writer's opinion – namely, that although the word (*tewa*, in old Hebrew) means ark, it can also mean language – is disputable, the highlighting of his discussion by citing Genesis (specifically, chapters 6-8 where Noah's story is told) is sound. In connection with the creation of human beings, one of the first things mentioned is language. Language and being human are thus seen as inextricably related. The confusion of tongues on the occasion of the building of the awesome tower of Babel (Gen. 11) expresses again the importance of language as well as disclosing one root cause of non-communication and abuse of science and technology, namely, pride.

have translated above as "overwhelming" because, whichever adjective is chosen, two of Descartes' ideas have had impressive positive and negative influence in the world of science, mathematics and philosophy.

As Hattori has pointed out on the first page of his essay, some of Descartes' methodology (not his later *cogito ergo sum*) has played a significant role in the development of many branches of the Tree of Wisdom (analogous to the Tree of Knowledge in Genesis). Indeed, in the annotated diagram of the tree he drew for me, he comments that on that pivotal night what Descartes caught a glimpse of was this Tree of Wisdom, not the *cogito sum*, "which comes later."

Concerning Descartes' negative influence we may ask, "Is doubt, as a form of psychological thinking that vanishes in a fleeting moment, compelling evidence for an enduring self?"

If Buddhism overemphasizes the discontinuous, ever fleeting, even non-existing "self," surely Westerners in the periods and places heavily influenced by Descartes have overemphasized the importance and endurance from moment to moment of the individual, isolated self.

We mustn't worry too long about where Descartes was when he had his major insight. However, the alternatives are fascinating. His words have suggested that he was sitting in a stove! Hattori chooses to see him in deep meditation alone in his room at an inn near Olm, seated in front of the fireplace. Another professor finds him in a "stove-heated tent (probably in a village near Ulm) in Germany on November 10, 1619, when Descartes was on his way from the coronation of Ferdinand II in Frankfurt to rejoin the army of Duke Maximilian"![4] *Where* he was pales in significance to *what* he was thinking, but the stove has remained a memorable image often found in the literature about Descartes.

The Note to Japanese readers is so important to us all that I shall excerpt some of its translation here:

> Descartes (1596-1650) regarded the whole universe that surrounds human beings as something like a precise clock . . . . He thought that anyone who carefully observes and analyzes such a universe can proceed to clear up whatever is mysterious. This way of thinking is spoken of as "a mechanistic world view." All of modern science is based on this thought, and in that sense Descartes is spoken of as the father of modern science.

While Hattori is keenly critical of the slavish adherence to certain aspects of Descartes' thought, he also feels that a door of his revelatory vision of Reason's potential has recently been opened wider by developments in physics:

> *At the core of what has recently turned up to oppose [more limiting perspectives] is the new science of quantum physics. Researchers in that field*

---

4. Quoted from a study guide (Copyright @ 1999 by Gerald J. Massey). Accessed 8-21-07 on the internet.

have pointed out that the "scientific failure" of classical physics lay in its complete separation of the observer from the observed. (There is no totally detached observer because the very act of observing helps determine what is seen.) This conclusion as expected is due to nothing so much as the "power of reason." Descartes had an inspired vision of that power.

7

An Apocalyptic World
Now it's time to think about Kant

Permanent peace must not arrive only on humanity's huge graveyard.[1]

"The second angel blew his trumpet, and something like a great mountain, burning with fire, was thrown into the sea. A third of the sea became blood, a third of the living creatures in the sea died, a third of the ships were destroyed." (Revelation 8:8-9)[2]

From about 2000 years later, newspaper accounts record striking parallels to the verses in the Apocalypse. Readers my find references to the flash of the A-bomb, the mountain-tall cloud, the change of the sea's color, the death of sea creatures, and the sinking of ships.

Is this remarkable agreement of what the book of Revelation says and what the modern press has reported merely an accident?

Whether one believes in Christianity or not, the biblical account contains teaching that is deeply significant. For example, we notice that the order of the

---

1. In this statement Immanuel Kant was referring to the satirical inscription on a Dutch innkeeper's sign depicting a graveyard under the words, PERPETUAL PEACE. See Kant, *Perpetual Peace*, ed. Lewis White Beck (New York: The Liberal Arts Press, 1957), 3.
2. Revelation, the last book of the Bible, is also known as the Apocalypse (from the transliteration of its Greek title). The word "apocalypse" has passed into English as a designation for doom or a series of catastrophically destructive events.

appearance of the earth and of life in Genesis is in rough accordance with present-day science. Human beings appear on earth as the recipients of life, and in the course of time soon become alienated from God.

In the Garden of Eden (Genesis 3) the serpent tells the woman that if she eats of the fruit of the tree she will become like God. The serpent did not deceive Eve but spoke the truth; human beings have become godlike. Lately the fruit of knowledge is the gigantic growth of science; soon humanity, by fabricating a system of values that places itself at the summit, will kill the Father God.[3]

Kyogō (arrogance) – this is the nub of the history of the human species. *Kyogō* is certainly about to lead to an abyss of destruction for mother earth. It escalates toward massacre on a global scale and becomes the conclusion of a history of alienation, that is, of various fractures in the relationships of people with nature and with each other. Furthermore, even tomorrow "winning" a nuclear war may produce synthetic monsters in the population because of "environmental hormones" that can affect people's reproductive capacity. Besides, smothered by various threats, the feelings of individuals will become paralyzed by inertia so that they will fail to respond appropriately.

> **Disowning God the Father**
>
> If one's concept of God, as dictated by modern culture, makes his existence irrelevant, at least our culture has killed the relevance of God, has it not?
>
> If on the other hand, we in some independence have somehow disowned the existing Father God, whether he's given up on people and this planet or not, we've "deaded" him to that extent, haven't we?
>
> Context is not *all*, but it is of critical importance. Even the Bible has the four words "There is no God." But see the context in Psalm 14:1.
>
> More context for Hattori's statement is found in the previous Encounter (Chapter 6) and elsewhere in the present book.

The Apocalypse of John tells about the end of the world as signaled by trumpets blown by seven angels. The third angel announces, "One-third of the sea has become wormwood, and many people have died from the water, because it has become bitter." (Rev. 8:11). Next, in the same manner, the fourth angel prophesies that "a third of the sun has become dark . . . ."

The United Nations has given notice that in 2025 an acutely serious shortage of sanitary drinking water will arise due to population increases and industrial

---

3. Hattori has a rather full discussion of this expression in *Letters from the Silk Roads*, Letter 11, "The Birth of Perspective." The letter closes with a reference to Nietzsche as author of the expression. For Austin Kline's brief but sound explication of Nietzsche's metaphor (sometimes quoted as "God is dead" and sometimes, as here, alluding to the "killing" of God), visit http://atheism.about.com/library/weekly/aa042600a.htm.

pollution. Isn't the following, as announced by the fifth angel, what certainly occurred in an underground experiment some years ago in India and Pakistan? "From the opening to the bottomless pit there arose smoke like the smoke of a great furnace, and the sun and air were darkened with the smoke from the opening." (Rev. 9:2)

Now, four countries on the perimeter of Mesopotamia, the cradle of civilization, either possess or are suspected of possessing nuclear weapons. In the Apocalypse, when the sixth angel blows his trumpet just before the end, the four angels who were bound to the great Euphrates River were released. They had been held ready "until that hour, day, month and year, to kill a third of humankind."

Two thousand years ago the author of Revelation predicted that this cosmic drama would unfold during a thirty-minute silence of the Lamb (Jesus) in Heaven.

As we view the things that have recently been occurring everywhere in our world, we surely need to focus our minds on the opening statement of UNESCO'S Constitution. "Since wars begin in the minds of men, it is in the minds of men that the defenses of peace must be constructed." This word stemmed from deep reflection on the part of the individuals gathered in 1945 amidst London's war damage. The problem of human consciousness has never been more clearly and positively put forth than in this utterance from the Constitution of UNESCO. So, representatives of the citizens of the world agreed to the statement. Besides, in the agreed-upon constitution it is clearly written, "that a peace based exclusively upon the political and economic arrangements of governments would not be a peace which could secure the unanimous, lasting and sincere support of the peoples of the world, and that the peace must therefore be founded, if it is not to fail, upon the intellectual and moral solidarity of mankind."

There is a pioneer who had already thought of this matter two centuries earlier – Immanuel Kant. "A peace treaty that secretly hides a reservation anticipating a future war must never be considered a peace treaty." Kant made this declaration in his little treatise *Perpetual Peace*,[4] and in it he surely took the sphere of the mind and its intentions seriously. What's more, he explained that for peace to prevail there must be "an end of all hostile intentions." Furthermore, all human acts, decisions, and policies directly causing wars must be renounced. So Kant had the same penetrating outlook as people working for UNESCO today – and this long before UNESCO was even created! "Standing armies shall in time be totally abolished." "No state shall by force interfere with the constitution or government of another country."[5] According to Kant, a state is like a living tree – with its own root system and its own claim to its soil – and also like a person, with the need

---

4. In the first section of *Perpetual Peace*, 3-4.
5. Preliminary Articles 3 and 5, pp. 5 and 7.

for respect and for being treated as being more than a mere means to another's happiness and welfare. In analogy with a stand-alone tree, one state must not try to graft another onto its trunk.[6]

Kant called this short book on peace, "my dream work." However, he believed that since he had this dream in the context of deep reflections about both politics and morality, it at least had the *possibility* of realization. He hoped for a day when daggers could be turned into tools to harvest grapes.

"Permanent peace must not arrive only on humanity's huge graveyard."

Bridge 7

Voice of a student: Dr. Hattori, would you please explain again to us younger folks what you think the Bible is telling us?

Hattori: Gladly, Davion! The gist of what I wrote for my Japanese readers may clarify matters for you.

Humanity has seated itself as God. As the serpent had predicted, "You'll be like God." This usurping of divine prerogatives exactly characterizes the modern period, so at last the word spoken by Nietzsche has come to pass, "God died." The modern destruction of the earth is an extension of that. The fact is that whether it's the Old or New Testament, we need to heed the warning of the end.

Davion: Dr. Gray, this reminds me of some sermons I've heard black preachers give more than the firefly metaphor you've chosen to emphasize.

Gray: You're paying attention! Hattori sometimes expresses himself as bluntly as John in Revelation or as a prophet in the Old Testament, but fireflies may warn each other of danger by flashing signals; those become their thunder and lightning!

Let's make a switch from the firefly hunt on familiar turf to a locale unfamiliar to all but the host guide. Imagine his tone of voice if a guest were about to fall into a rushing stream or go over an innocent-looking cliff.

Davion: He'd be loud and urgent.

Gray: Exactly! There are several cliffs toward which we humans are straying perilously close. Let's consider one. Do you as a young person have any particular concerns about the increasing violence in our world?

Davion: Yes, I do have concerns. I have found the book of Revelation to be a very intriguing Biblical book. Upon reading it, I see that many of images found there may have become historical happenings or possibly will still literally happen in the future. That gives me chills.

---

6. Article 2, p. 4.

I have recently been paying more attention to politics, economics, and world news in general. Every day it seems as if evil's grip on the world is getting slightly tighter. I hear of oil prices rising, terrorist groups increasing in number and intensity, the proliferation of nuclear weapons, and threats from overpopulation. Most of these problems could be resolved, but I strongly believe that many of the most powerful people on this earth are not men of God (or even of the gods) but rather men of greed causing others to suffer.

8

The Holy Mother Ascends
The Sea and Life

In the human gene, which has transited five million years of time, there is presumed to be written the memory of life born in the sea 3.8 billion years ago. What emerges in my mind as I stand in front of that sea is the appearance of the earth itself in remote ages.

I've just found it!
– What? – Eternity.
It is sea that is mixed and merged with the sun.[1]

This verse is from one of Arthur Rimbaud's last poems as recorded in his collection, *A Season in Hell*. This poet was extraordinarily talented; however, at age twenty, he abandoned poetry and professional writing. When I gazed at the sunset while the sun was slowly sinking and tinting the Aegean Sea gold, this particular passage from *A Season in Hell* came to mind. I was looking at the sunset from a cliff on Santorin, the island in the eastern Mediterranean that hides[2] the legend of the vanished country of Atlantis.

---

1. This is Hattori's and my paraphrase from the French *Une Saison en enfer*, originally published by Rimbaud personally in 1873. (At last sighting that version in its original packaging was available on the WWW for $38,000.)
2. I wondered why Hattori speaks of the Atlantis legend as being hidden until I remembered that fabled Atlantis is supposed to lie somewhere to the *west* of the Gates of Gibraltar. If in actual fact it existed to the *east* of Gibraltar, its identity has been *hidden* from usual

The island Santorin (or, Santorini) known as Thira or Thera in ancient times, was connected to Crete by waters stretching only 75 miles (100 km) southward from Santorin. Due to great eruptions in 1700 B.C. and 1500 B.C., the island was largely buried in the sea. Now only a small half-moon shaped island remains. Clinging to a steep cliff at the rim of the volcano's crater there is the beautiful white village of Fira. The scene it presents is unlike any other in the world. Isn't it a figure for humanity's precarious clinging to planet Earth? In fact, that one huge explosion of long ago destroyed the preeminent Minoan civilization that antedated Greek civilization. The eruption is estimated to have had the force of 2,000 bombs of the kind dropped on Hiroshima.

"The ocean itself is the most beautiful evidence from the great past of the Mediterranean. I like to tell that story, I like to tell it again and again. One must see the ocean. And one needs to see it repeatedly." In the 20th century Fernand Braudel (1902-1985), who brought about a reform in studies of comparative civilizations, began his "*Les mémoires de la Méditerranée*"[3] with the words just quoted. He continues: "Isn't the sea itself a mother? Oh, come to think of it, the word *la mer* (sea) can, because of its identical pronunciation in French, pass for the word *la mère* (mother). – Then perhaps, Poseidon is not god of the sea but of storms of the sea."

The appearance of the world in remote times emerges for me as I stand on the shore in front of the sea – a sea that changes every morning and every evening, its deep blues speaking to the soul.

If we think of "remote times" in terms of tens of millions of years, even Europe was reborn from the ocean. The island of Crete, Greece, and, yes, also the Atlas Mountains (named after the god who supports the canopy of heaven) as they stand at the north to northwestern edge of Africa, as well as Mt. Olympus, the residence of gods, and even the Alps and Caucasus Mountains – all these were birthed from a primordial sea.

> Five thousand years ago the goddess of fertility appeared on the banks of the river Indus, and no more than three thousand years ago the father god above appeared in Israel and Greece. In the human gene, which has transited five million years of time, there is presumed to be written the memory of life born in the sea 3.8 billion years ago. Therefore, even now when I view the sea, I feel a sense of relief . . . . [4]

---

conversation and speculation. In *Micropaedia* it is stated that if Plato did not invent the story, it "may in fact reflect ancient Egyptian records of a volcanic eruption on the island of Thera about 1500 BC."

3. Published posthumously in 1988. I believe the rest of this page blends Hattori's reflections with Braudel's *mémoires*.
4. "Relief" is a literal translation, perhaps with a hint of being at peace with time's immensity.

Beneath my gaze stood Santorin's unique church of the blue-dome. The bell built into the arch at the top of the church was sending forth its peals over the sea. They invited my mind and heart to revisit the church of Santa Marie do la Mer (St. Mary of the Sea) where Saint Mary was worshipped in the south of France at a site sacred to Gypsies.

"It's the same over there," I thought. "The statues of Mary were washed ashore from the sea."

The Gothic churches in the north of medieval Europe had needle-like spires that looked exactly as if they were pointing toward heaven. That was suggestive of someone praying with arms extended toward God the Father. However, for the traveler in southern France, there is something that will surely strike the eye. If you go down toward the Mediterranean, the Gothic spires tend to disappear the farther south you go. In place of them the number of churches lifting their bell towers progressively increases. One also notices the appearance of the statue of the Holy Mother at the apex of each church. The very soul of Christianity is found in the crucifixion of Jesus as symbolized by a cross. However, Renaissance artists de-emphasized this precedent and priority. They came to favor the Holy Mother. In that time when they rediscovered the beauty of humanity, surely the affection expressed by the artists in their paintings and statues of the Holy Mother included praise for the infant Jesus. However, that is not the whole story. It has been proven that, already in the area southwest of Paris in the pre-Renaissance Chartres Cathedral (13th century), the statue of Black Mary, which was the most revered image at that time, is the same goddess worshipped in Druidism before the introduction of Christianity, as goddess of fertility.

This goddess of life approaches the South or the area of sun and sea and passes right through the chancel of the dim churches to the outside, and there she ascends to their roofs. Consider two sites on the Mediterranean – Sète and Marseilles. The azure sea glittering with sunlight was celebrated by that eminent poet Valéry, whose birthplace was Sète. Sète overlooks the harbor at Massalia, modern Marseilles, first constructed by the Greeks. In such places the images of the Holy Mother still attract intent gazes. Sailors returning to Marseilles from far-away oceans can recognize from a distance the statue of the Holy Mother that stands on the roof of the Church of Notre Dame do la Charledo. When they do, they sigh with relief, "Ah! We're back." Even if we go to China, we find a goddess

---

A MARRIAGE?
Father God with the Sea Goddess!

My best understanding is that Rimbaud's line of poetry, as repeated in this essay, adumbrates the merging of the energy-emitting sun with the sometimes placid waters of the sea. The metaphor suggests a feminine reception of masculine insemination.

A different but related polarity is that between the peaceful sea and its all too stormy catastrophes – and, we might add, between the ancient virgin Mother and more recent Fatherly Deities. – WG

of the sea, Matsu. Her festivals have dotted the eastern coast of China.

The few frescoes that are left in Santorin overflow with depictions of vegetation and fish celebrating the joy of life. As I watched the sun sink into the Aegean Sea, I recalled the boundless whirlpool I had seen on Crete. That whirlpool churns with a vast memory of life. The goddess of fertility whom the earth embraces as the source of life is revived and linked once more with the primordial sea that gave birth to life's story by its mingling with the sun.[5]

Bridge 8

Hattori speaking:

> In the spring of 1999, I returned to Greece with a special seminar of Reitaku University students. At that time, because of the distances involved, we took in only one island, Santorin, where we could look down from a steep cliff on the sun as it sank into the Aegean. The students with me seemed to feel deep emotion as they watched that sunset.

The brilliant poet Rimbaud lived and died in the 19th century (1854-1891), and yet the reverberations of his strange and often repulsive life and work had effects in art, lifestyles, philosophy, and general innovation far beyond his time. Of him Peyre says, "Rimbaud is, along with Victor Hugo, the most imaginative of French poets."

I've forgotten from what source I learned this, but, although Rimbaud was an important influence for French symbolist artists, he had an even greater impact on Dadaists and Surrealists.[6] His life and the products of his imagination remind us, not so much of science and order, as of chaos and destruction (as in the biblical book of Revelation or in recent chaos theory). While his lifestyle and literary style antedate the Beats in late 20th century literature and certain Rap lyricists in the 21st, he was also, according to translator Peschel, "the human factor that led [Paul Claudel] back to his Catholic faith." Furthermore, while he sometimes arrogantly claimed to disdain and transcend even the greatest of the French poets, in his humbler moments he acknowledged his indebtedness to poets such as Victor Hugo. He called *Les Misérables* "a true poem."

* * *

---

5. Compare the churning sea of milk in Chapter 28 for similar intimations of the cycles of destruction/construction.
6. Here and in what follows I am relying on several sources, but most of what I say is confirmed or elaborated by the excellent essay on Rimbaud in the *Micropedia* portion or the 2007 *New Encyclopaedia Britannica*. – WG

Now I'd like to ask my mentee a question.

"Davion, I tried in the boxed text on the sea goddess or goddesses to connect several seemingly disconnected topics. Do you think I succeeded?"

"Wow! That box contains a mouthful! It tells me that the divine may include sexuality and gender in its nature. I thought such features had to be excluded. . ."

"Well, Davion, in one respect you're right. Such a way of thinking of God is the *via negative*, because it emphasizes what God is *not*. However, the positive way emphasizes what God is *like*; it is metaphoric. My box is filled with metaphor.

9

Earth's Dignity
Visiting Greece in the Springtime

> Ruins present their own style of beauty, do they not? In the deepest reaches of the human heart, the beauty of ruins must somehow intermesh with the heart's desire for eternity.

I once gained a vivid impression from the white path ascending a certain hill. The pillars that towered between the mountains belonged to the shrine of Apollo of Delphi. At that time I was a student at the Sorbonne, and even now I remember the dazzling impression of light from the just-risen sun. In Greece springtime is the season that arises in spite of whether one utters words such as "springtime," "Dionysius"[1] or "coming to life again." When the winter rain clouds dissipate and sunlight returns to the Aegean, even the breezes seem to shine and flowers begin to blossom all at once. Flowers adorn the fresh verdure of the valleys so that they look like a piece of brocade.

Blossoms burst forth around Easter. In this season I wanted to let students see the sacred place of the god of light, Apollo; that was my hope. If you look down from a height, beneath your eyes appears a sea of the olive trees' silvery foliage spreading limitlessly in front of you. The olive tree is a Greek symbol. In Greece of long ago, Poseidon, the sea god, fought for the land that became Athens; in

---

1. God of fruitfulness and vegetation, wine and ecstasy.

that fight he struck the soil with his trident and made salt water gush forth. To counteract this, the goddess of wisdom, Athena – the very one who is said to have sprung forth in gold armor from the head of Zeus! – stuck her spear into the earth and caused the first olive tree to appear. The gods who approved of this gift gave the Acropolis to Athena and thus made her the city's patron and protector.

The land of Greece is not at all fertile. Its soil is full of rocks; it is dry and hard to cultivate. So in that place people came to clear the land and plant olive trees. Then, as soon as a food supply was assured, culture emerged for the first time. Agriculture (tilling the soil) is culture's partner.

A Greek pillar soars; it's a nature-defying *declaration of man*! When I first looked up at the Delphic shrine of Apollo, deep emotions passed through my heart. In these holy precincts on a steep mountainside I found indications of what human beings in peak form can build, including as many as possible of the basic institutions that constitute communities: neighborhood shrines, circular theaters for the exposition of the arts and sciences, and places for the games and contests related to physical training, to mention just a few examples. In museum displays we can feel humanity as it moves and acts with beauty in the step by step expression of the human spirit. We may even feel a synthesis of Egyptian quietude and Oriental "soul."

However, how did the "oracular" word happen to be uttered here? This oracle at Apollo's shrine informed Socrates that he was the wisest of all men. In the midst of deep doubt about this, Socrates became aware of something. It was the fact that, as he says, "Other men are not aware of their ignorance. However, I myself know that I know nothing." The extent to which the Oracle of Delphi was respected may be understood from the fact that in every division of this Greek city there were built treasure halls for the consecration of offerings to it.

The people who had spent a day purifying their bodies in ritual baths in the circular shrine at the foot of the mountain, next morning climbed the hill with the sunlight and received an oracle from a shrine maiden of Apollo. However, before Apollo came here, this was the site for the oracle of Gaea, the goddess of earth. Delphi was even made the center of the earth by Zeus, and the rock there continues to be associated with Gaea's navel. This holy place was protected by Python. Even after Python was defeated by Apollo and "replaced" by him, the shrine virgins in the inner sanctum were known as Pythian maidens and were believed to inhale the "soul" of the steam gushing forth from the bowels of the earth deep beneath the shrine. They thereby became mediums for immediate transmission of the oracle's prophecies.

All this encapsulates important human 10th century BC history for the area: the arrival from the north of the Greeks, who worshiped the gods of Mt. Olympus along with the heavenly god Zeus, ruling over all from its peak. Around 1000 BC, the Minoan civilization was born on the island of Crete in the far-off Aegean Sea. Moreover, there was the not disconnected existence of the Mycenaean civilization on the Peloponnesian Peninsula, a civilization that helped transmit

Minoan civilization northward. All of these influences were assimilated into the successor Greek civilization. The earth goddess Python, who was worshipped by the Greeks where they had previously lived, had her antecedent in those ancient civilizations. Also, Athena, Zeus's daughter, is perceived as having surely been a metamorphosis of the reptile Python, now assuming an owl-like form – like the owl of Minerva.

Whenever I stand before ruins, I feel that the vast history of humankind is therein condensed. The beauty of ruins is the "beauty of time." Once, in a little gem of a composition entitled, "The Dignity of the Earth," Takeo Kuwabara, a leader in Kyoto who was deeply involved in UNESCO, spoke these words:

> As for monuments that have survived till today more than a thousand years later, we may say that by their very grandeur they have transcended their regional and ethnic limitations: they take us toward their original idea. Today the Chartres Cathedral, the Blue Mosque, Angkor Wat – all alike, whether they are Buddhist, Christian, or Islamic, evoke a feeling of being wrapped in beauty. Such creations typify the birth of a global sense of beauty, and so the strong point of works that are supremely aesthetic is continually rediscovered by self-conscious, mature citizens of Earth.

What must we young men have been thinking when we trod the white path that ascends the hill of the Acropolis? How were we affected by the circular theater of Epidaurus – or by our viewing of the palace of Gnosis?

When the human heart is moved not only by the beauty of ruins but also by the "beauty of time," there is a deep feeling akin to the hope for eternity hidden in the human breast. Even though that feeling assumes a variety of forms, the perceptions are interlinked. At rock bottom, isn't what is being perceived simply beauty pure and timeless?

Now cultural assets are being destroyed by racial and ethnic disputes. In such times as these, there is all the more reason for us to saturate ourselves in the global heritage we share on this planet. Working toward preserving the cultural heritage through international cooperation nurtures what a scholar has spoken of as "an awareness of beauty globally." Efforts that cross religious and ethnic barriers may become the only kind of coordinated action that builds profound social and inner peace.

Bridge 9

The theme sentence for this encounter is remarkably reminiscent of the English poet William Wordsworth's ode, "Intimations of Immortality from Recollections of Early Childhood." Note especially these lines from that ode:

> The sunshine is a glorious birth;
> But yet I know, where'er I go,

> That there has passed away a glory from the earth. . . .
> Our birth is but a sleep and a forgetting:
> The Soul that rises with us, our life's Star,
> Hath had elsewhere its setting,
> And cometh from afar. . . .
> But trailing clouds of glory do we come
> From God, who is our home:
> Heaven lies about us in our infancy!

What Wordsworth attributes to youthful sensitivity to all that exists, is the very thing that Hattori finds in the infancy of the world and even in history's ruins.

In the introduction to his poem, Wordsworth speaks of "communing" with all that he saw as a child and learning again to use this gift as an adult.

WG: Davion, you might like to think of what you as a young adult are learning to value from your childhood and, now, from your work in English literature. Let's reflect a little on another example, a portion of John Keats' famous poem . . .

> A thing of beauty is a joy for ever:
> Its loveliness increases; it will never
> Pass into nothingness; but still will keep
> A bower quiet for us, and a sleep
> Full of sweet dreams, and health, and quiet breathing.

In your effort to step away from macho insensitivity toward beauty, love, responsibility and concern for others, can you, Davion, come up with anything comparable in pop culture to Wordsworth or Keats?

Davion: Yes, Dr. Gray, I can give an modest example, but first I want to say that this whole chapter paints a vivid picture of gods rising from the ruins, especially the ones left over from the battle between Poseidon and Athena. It must have been a wonderful experience to be right there where the Greek gods still reigned religiously and then later, in poetic and philosophical imagination. The mysterious quality of the people who once worshiped these gods fascinates me.

Also, Socrates' rising above the quest for specialized, success-driven "knowledge" inspires me. As a 22-year-old male, I am impressed by his search for the knowledge of goodness. That search must have also impressed the oracle of Delphi. Maybe it is wise sometimes for us Americans to admit we have a lot of information but lack wisdom and even basic morality.

Also, when I read John Keats' poem, it makes me think of a song entitled "Zion" by Lauryn Hill, a critically acclaimed black singer. This song focuses on the beauty of her newborn son, Zion, and how her past joys gave place to joy for her newborn.

10

"Quo Vadis, Domine?"
People Who Have Seen God

One day, spontaneously, a love beyond duty sprang up in her heart as proof she had met God.

The Christmas season is a time when many and various thoughts run through our minds about the passing years:

In sharp contrast to the sad splendor of Princess Diana's funeral, was Mother Teresa's that immediately followed it but was permeated by solemnity. What especially moved me was the fact that not only Christians but Hindus, Buddhists, and Muslims – all these, rising above sectarian divisions, came to express one mind in their shared condolences. If we consider the fact that condolences came from India's Punjab state, as well as such nations as Sri Lanka, Northern Ireland, Bosnia, Algeria, and Kosovo, in all of which a disastrous shedding of blood has been perpetrated in the name of religion, this interreligious respect for Mother Teresa is all the more astounding.

Throughout her life, she united her mind with that of the Supreme One, who can be discovered in the depths of the human mind though it changes its name to Deus, Allah, Brahma, God, Kami, and Buddha. She had discovered the divine mind in the profundity of the human heart. I think everyone respects a person from whose heart emanate deeds of compassion transcending ordinary life. Widespread respect naturally caused her funeral to be a trans-religious state funeral or even a world funeral.

One day, spontaneously, a love beyond duty sprang up in her heart as proof that she had met God. It emerged in the form of compelling actions as she bravely gave herself to extending a helping hand to people in all kinds of trouble and desperate need. She built houses or centers for the blind, aged, and lepers in Calcutta and in some extremely poor developing countries. They were named Homes of Heart-Healing and Hospices for Peaceful Death. This was the act of a true Christian. "True" here refers to something *universal*, because it is felt to be true by all human beings. However, the way to reach the universal is indeed a strict and rigorous way.

At the end of the masterpiece *Quo Vadis*, which depicts the followers of Christ in the period of the Roman Empire, there is a scene that I would summarize as follows.[1]

Peter, as the cornerstone of Christ's church, has received from Jesus the greatest responsibility of any disciple. Now, unable to bear the continual persecution of those who follow Christ, he at last is running away from Rome. As he trudges along the Appian Way toward the mountain pass, he sees a figure approaching him. When the figure gets close, Peter realizes it is Jesus, the one who has already died on the cross in faraway Jerusalem. In wonderment he asks, "*Quo vadis, Domine?*" (Lord, where are you going?), and Christ answers in a sadly sweet voice that Peter can only hear as severe, "If you abandon my people, I am going to Rome to be crucified a second time."

Peter, thunderstruck, jumps to his feet and turns back to Rome, where he proceeds to await his own death.[2] However, in due time the very Rome that killed him is going to accept Christianity as the state religion of the empire, and the world is going to change greatly.

The voice of a deliverer once in a while becomes a thunderous roar. At certain other times it becomes a great serene and steady river that sustains and protects us when our minds are sinking into confusion and we feel like lost sheep. At the beginning of the 20th century, the eminent spiritual leader Chikuro Hiroike (founder of the moral philosophy he termed "Moralogy") discovered a common basis for supreme morality in all of the world religions. In his last days Hiroike left a saying that went something like this. "My heart is filled by sincere wishes to save people; now I let everything of my own belong to God; I let my own body and soul belong to the light, the light of God's wisdom, in other words, the light of mercy; and I feel as if I live under divine protection. . . ."

---

1. *Quo Vadis* made its Polish author, Henryk Sienkiewiez, internationally famous. His novels on Polish history earned him the Nobel Prize for Literature in 1905. *Quo Vadis* has been filmed five times over a period extending from 1909 to 2001.
2. Sienkiewiez (518) elaborates, "He walked with solemn attention, but with calmness, feeling that since the death on Golgotha nothing equally important had happened, and that as the first death had redeemed the whole world, this was to redeem the city."

This word reminds us of the following words of Paul (Galatians 2:20), who constructed the foundation of Christian theology. "It is no longer I who live, but it is Christ who lives in me." People who say things like this have in common an intuitive feeling that whatever acts as the foundation of the universe is not a cold, stationary point but a living love that is Life itself.

They give themselves to it and at the same time lend their hands to others. In Buddhism what we are speaking of is the core meaning of Maitreya and *jin* (仁), that is to say, benevolence.[3]

Whoever lives this way is no other than a bodhisattva.[4] The Buddha as Truth does not remain a goal to be reached but is constantly transforming himself into Bodhisattva in order to save people suffering from 108 desires. Bodhisattva's thousand hands reach out to help them. This compassionate aspect of the Bodhisattva is seen in all the world religions. In that sense Mother Teresa's single lifetime was the same kind of vehicle as any other bodhisattva sailing along on a lotus blossom of compassion. The God in whom she believed was the one whose son had to be sent to earth by the God of love for the expiation of sin and for the rescue of human beings from their deserved condemnation.

God is omnipresent. This God has personally approached humanity. That means God has made human beings in his image, and no matter how wicked a person is, each of us lodges something divine in a corner of our heart, even if it's in a very small corner. The Bodhisattva has both an upward movement that points toward limitless Truth and an unlimited descent to save humanity.

In the novel *Fukai Kawa (Deep River)*, Shūsako Endō tells of a student of theology, Ōtsu, who is frustrated by a cultural gap in the churches of the West. While bearing a body to a cremation site on the banks of the Ganges in Varanasi

---

3. Sidney Brown points out that this character is composed of "man" on the left and "two" on the right and so incorporates the idea of two persons interacting. When I checked Hattori's Japanese in the original, I found that he used a much more complicated term (*ji*, 慈 21 strokes!) meaning compassion or benevolence. A key part of this character is "heart." Without tutoring me in *ji* (the verb is pronounced *itsukushimu*), Hattori allowed me to use the same meaning as suggested by Brown and the 4-stroke 仁. A baseball idiom reassures the three of us with our varying terms and meanings, "You're all in the same ballpark!"
4. Maitreya (Miroku in Japanese) is the Buddha-to-come. The name may be an echo of Hindu and Persian deities. In the southern form of Buddhism, Buddha is thought to have predicted a decline of religion and morality so that Maitreya must come to set things right. In Mahayana, the northern version, Maitreya is most emphatically a bodhisattva in the sense that Western readers and devotees most admire. Bodhisattvas are models of other-concern. They defer their own enlightenment until all other creatures are saved. Because they thus sacrifice their own good for others, "they are popularly called upon for help." See Geoffrey Parrinder's *A Dictionary of Non-Christian Religions* (Philadelphia: The Westminster Press, 1971), 48.

(Benares), at last the seminarian has a spark of insight: "God, like the layers of an onion that never stop being onion, never stops being God but is everywhere. God is the warmth of life."

The Absolute can be invoked by any name.

Bridge 10

Hattori elaborates:

> What is referred to as the "bodhisattva way" or "bodhisattva's vehicle"[5] means that during one's search for truth, one must extend a helping hand to others. This is the most marvelous thought that can be found in Mahayana Buddhism. From the start, the Mahayana Bodhisattva would extend help to people no one else notices and even to wicked people as well. One who acts thus is a bodhisattva, but in the division of Buddhism honored as the Way of the Elders (Theravada or Hinayana) there is nothing called a bodhisattva. For a lay person in Theravada to give alms to a priest is not the same as the bodhisattva way, because in Theravada, almsgiving promotes the sharing of monkish virtues and only helps the giver gain escape from hell or the lower rebirths.
>
> However, although Mahayana is conceptually superior, in modern Japan this branch of Buddhism suffers from many problems of practice. Since Hinayana adheres more strictly to the Teachings, it is respected for acting strictly by original Buddhist tradition.
>
> What Christianity preaches – namely, that, like the shepherd, God and his servants always seek the lost lamb – is also Mahayana's teaching. This is the same situation as the teaching in Mahayana Buddhism that the bodhisattva extends a helping hand to the stupid, the wicked, and the overlooked. In this sense, I think that both Mahayana Buddhism and Christianity arrive at the same conclusion.
>
> Chikuro Hiroike, as hinted above, has explained the logical thread uniting Christ, Buddha, Socrates, and Confucius.

* * *

---

5. The spelling convention in English permits either "Bodhisattva" or "bodhisattva." But the shifting from one to the other in this Bridge has a more specific meaning. "Bodhisattva" (with a capital B) emphasizes the transcendent element – the peak of our best or the peak even beyond our merely human best.

WG: Now, Davion, we'd like to ask you as a young adult, to give your response to this way of thinking.

Davion: I find the term bodhisattva very interesting and personally relevant. For the past couple of years I've found myself helping individuals that many other people would not deal with because of socioeconomic or ethnic bias – or plain ignorance of these others.

I enjoy helping people progress and improve different aspects of their lives. For example, there is a young man who attends this same college. He's originally from the Chicago area and acts kind of out of place in the small community of Winfield, Kansas. He seems rather goofy, because he doesn't have a sense of appropriate dress or appearance, so I encourage him to shave regularly and keep a sharper image of himself mentally and physically. I can see that he is slowly but surely picking up speed. At times he uses his natural charisma to progress in his relationships with other people, despite the unfamiliar setting. This is gratifying to me.

11

Way to China
The Route Napoleon Lost

From the 16th to the 18th centuries, what every European country was aiming at was Asia and especially China. The reason was that China indeed was the world's most advanced country and produced the most exceptionally fine goods.

There is an arch that is slender and beautiful and that defines a great empty space. I saw it shining with its silvery sparkle as it reared its apex 192 meters (630 ft.) on its spot beside the mighty Mississippi River. The Gateway Arch was built in 1967 as a monument to commemorate the place from which the pioneers departed towards the western part of the U.S.A. Seen from afar, it seems unbelievable that a gondola could climb up inside the triangular cross-section of arch. When we have boarded one of the gondolas and ridden to the top of the arch, then through the small windows we may catch a view of the vast panorama. Turning one way we can see the state of Missouri and, in the opposite direction, the state of Illinois.

In the underground theater beneath this arch I saw the 70mm movie, *The Great American West* projected on a giant-screen. It began in French.

The year is 1803, and the place is Napoleon's residence in Paris. There a report is being conveyed by the Minister of Foreign Affairs who has just arrived by coach. The person sitting in the office with his back to us, as though absorbed in thought, is young Napoleon Bonaparte. This is just prior to the time when he becomes emperor. He has already integrated most of Europe with the exception of Britain. The news that has now arrived is to the effect that the American President Jefferson has agreed to the Louisiana Purchase for the sum of $15,000,000.

Saying, "Your Excellency has emptied Jefferson's purse," the minister is just getting up to leave when Napoleon detains him with, "Just a minute!"

Napoleon is examining a large but incomplete map. "There is something that I have been thinking about for some time. I have been wondering whether or not there may be a route through there to the West."

"I think that is impossible," replies the minister.

So the movie goes. I do not know how accurate this exchange is. However, it is probably fairly close to the truth. At this time Napoleon did not know what he had lost. And at that moment history was in the process of being significantly altered.

French Louisiana happened to be truly a vast territory crossing America diagonally from the Southeast to the Pacific Coast on the northwest of North America. In fact, it now occupied more than a third of the whole United States of America.

Jefferson, despite congressional opposition, had pushed through the purchase of this territory, and now proceeded right away to dispatch two young men, Lewis and Clark, up the Missouri River – from the confluence of the Missouri and Mississippi rivers – to explore the interior of this purchase. Proceeding upstream, crossing wastelands, obtaining the cooperation of the native peoples, at length they and their support team of persons with a variety of skills both technical/practical and linguistic/cultural finally reached the Rocky Mountain Range and opened a path to the American Pacific. The question as to whether there was a passage to the West suggests to me that perhaps Napoleon was also considering this to be a distinct possibility.

Now, we must look back on history. When Queen Isabella of Castile sponsored Columbus' 1492 expedition to cross the Atlantic, it was never intended to lead to the discovery of a "New World." When Columbus, convinced that the earth was round, sailed westward, his objectives were India, Cathay (China), and Jipangu (Japan). Due to the mistaken notion that he and his colleagues had arrived in India, they called the islands and their vicinity the West Indies and their longtime native residents, Indians.

From the 16th to the 18th century, what all European nations were aiming at was Asia, especially China. The reason is that China was indeed the most advanced nation in the world because of its production of excellent goods. All countries were seeking trade with China. The eminent Dutch scholar Andre Gunder Frank addressed the International Society for the Comparative Study of Civilizations meeting in St. Louis in 1999. On that occasion he overturned the commonly accepted theory that the period beginning with the 16th century was one characterized by Europe's preeminence in the world. Of this he said, "In the 18th century, the Gross Domestic Product for China (GDP) was three times that of Europe." Frank pointed to the fact that in China silver was being accumulated from the whole world, including Japan. In particular, the silver discovered in the New World was being used to buy Chinese products.

"Europe only gained a dominant position in the 19th century." This announcement by Professor Frank does run against common opinion, but his argument is persuasive.[1] Nevertheless, Japan is scarcely included in this cogent revision of history, although the Iwami silver mine was producing one-third of the world's silver needs at that time. It is a fact that while Europe was planning to overturn the axis of the world system through its "industrial revolution," Japan was in the midst of an "industrious revolution." In other words, through economization and recycling, Japan took off from[2] China in a way similar to what Europe did. Soon after this, Japan experienced the Meiji Restoration.[3]

While still using the Indian sea route to the East, Europe was seeking a westward route to Asia. When it became known that the New World was not India or China, Spain baptized Mexico *Nueva España*, "New Spain." The ships that departed from the harbor at Acapulco on the Pacific Coast headed west to load Chinese products in Manila, and having turned north to ride the Kuroshio or Black Current, returned to their home port. These ships were called Manila Galleons. This trade at one time gave Spain a preeminent position among European nations. Was not the first American "opening of the West" the pioneer expansion to the Pacific, and was not the object of its second expansion Asia? The expropriation of Hawaii and the Philippines confirms this idea.

If his minister had answered, "Yes, I think so," when Napoleon wondered aloud whether there might be a new route to China, history might have taken a completely different course.

Bridge 11

A significant historical fact is that Queen Isabella of Castile (1451-1504) "and her counselors were more ready to recognize the rights of the Indians than was Columbus; she ordered some of those he had brought back as slaves to be released." (*Micropaedia*, Vol. 6, "Isabella I," p. 398.)

A historically disputable point concerns Japan's economic take-off. Woodburn and other Euro-American historians believe this was "triggered by [Japan's] being forced open to outside trade by American gunboats."

Hattori responds, "This comes later. Europeans' misunderstanding is to think this opening was the beginning of Japanese development. Japan *did develop* during

---

1. History professor Stephen Woodburn of Southwestern College concurs but adds that China had no similar goal of its own. "Europe, a fractious region, turned competition into an engine of progress. . . . China had no one to catch up to."
2. *Ririku suru*, meaning in this case to leave something swiftly behind.
3. The dispute surrounding this point is due in part to the different rates at which historians assimilate cutting-edge research such as Dr. Frank's.

the Edo (Tokugawa) period, lasting from about 1600 to 1867." Many experts on Japan and world economics are tending to agree with Hattori's conclusion about this.[4]

For many Americans, Hattori's statement that Asia was an object of the second wave of expansion to the West may come as a surprise if not an occasion for skepticism.

However, here what Dr. Woodburn has communicated to me may be of special interest:

> The seizure of the Philippines and Hawaii were part of the rush for colonies in the run-up to World War I, in which all nations aspiring to prominence took part. Puerto Rico and Cuba were part of this effort, justified by security needs for forward bases in all directions. Your author [Hattori] might be interested in the 1898 speech, later a bestselling pamphlet, "The March of the Flag" by Albert J. Beveridge, which proclaimed that the oceans (because of naval capabilities in the industrial age) made such overseas territories "contiguous."

---

4. For a brief but telling exposition of rapidly changing recent research on this, see Robert B. Marks' review of *Growth Recurring: Economic Change in World History* (University of Michigan Press, 2000) for the *Journal of World History* (Spring 2002), 190-192

12

Writing the Future
Kaii Higashiyama's Memorable Poster, "The Road"

> The past is already written. It cannot be changed. However, we can write the future.
>
> – Federico Mayor

There are select moments that influence a whole lifetime. One such moment I vividly recall was when Federico Mayor, on a day at the outset of 1988, swept up to the platform to assume office as the new Director General of UNESCO. I had the profound feeling that a flash of the sun's light had come to fill a sky overcast by dark clouds.

In 1984, America and then Britain in '85, criticized UNESCO because its leader at that time was the Director General, Amadou M'Bow of Senegal. The two countries withdrew from this UN agency saying it was promoting "restriction of freedom of the press," "politicization of the organization," and "mismanagement." That is to say, UNESCO had leaned too far toward the Soviet Union, and Third World countries were aligning themselves with Soviet-dominated Eastern Europe. America, which took pride in its world leadership, was calculating the unseating of Mr. M'Bow. Instead of yielding to his critics, Mr. M'Bow opposed them face to face. In his opposition to America and Britain, Mr. Mbow, who was a star of hope for the Third World, was far from yielding to the other side. He flatly rejected the criticisms aimed at him. Furthermore, his position, even if eclipsed by voices of concern about the financial crisis arising due to American withdrawal from UNESCO, was not totally invalidated; he remained a needed advocate for the majority of developing nations that had in common a number of jeopardized interests. Against this background, Mr. M'Bow in 1987 announced he was going to run for the third time for the office of Director General of UNESCO. Several Western powers and various countries including Japan began to follow the example of America and Britain. This constituted a crisis for UNESCO.

However, in September of 1987 Federico Mayor of Spain was finally elected by the Executive Board. It was a hard struggle from the first of six ballots in the first round of voting. (There were five rounds). Mayor had already gained experience as the Deputy Director General of UNESCO, as President of Granada University, and as the Minister of Education in Spain. This young and handsome biologist from Catalonia, Spain, lacked the backing of his own country's government. Even without it, he was able to become a candidate thanks to a signature-writing campaign sponsored by a number of scholarly societies in Europe and America.

There is a custom that a new Director General will formally address his entire staff. On such occasions, M'Bow had always surrounded himself with his close collaborators such as the assistant director generals.[1] However, that day Mayor appeared by himself on a totally bare stage. In his hand was only one small book – UNESCO's charter. What a fresh approach! He made expert use of three languages – first French, next English, and lastly Spanish. Without handing the staff any printed materials, he simply began to chat with them. At the end of his presentation, the Nobel-prize poet Pablo Neruda rounded off the session with the following poem:

> Even if all the roses are cut down in our garden,
> That will not prevent the return of spring.

Mayor was a man with whom many on the staff felt they could get along.

When he was Undersecretary of UNESCO, I had already had the chance to observe and admire his characteristics. Consequently, now that he was head of the secretariat, I confidently proposed projects and programs, for example, a whole series of seminars on topics such as, "Dialogue of Science with Culture," "An Integral Study of Silk Roads: Roads of Dialogue," "A Paris-Japan Festival,"

---

1. Hattori explains his use in this context of the Japanese word *hinadan* (stage or gallery) which I have left out of my translation. The word evokes for Japanese readers an image of a common type of home display at the time of the annual Girls Day festival. Each display is full of puppets with the Emperor in the center – an authoritarian figure surrounded by his retinue. In Hattori's usage here, the term alludes ironically to the presence on stage of M'Bow's lieutenants. (By the way, Hattori uses "puppet" in its very secondary sense of "dolls" in American English. He avoids using "dolls," because these figures are not toys to play with as much as for viewing. Anyone, not just a child, may appreciate them. When my wife and I were in a doctor's home in Kitakyushu for a medical appointment, we were invited into a special room to view the daughter's display. She was at the time a university student.)

and "A Declaration of the Rights of Future Generations" (related to the global environment). If we were able to achieve good results from these projects, it was because of the deep mutual confidence implicit in our relationship.

However, time flew like an arrow, and Federico Mayor, having already completed two terms in office over a twelve-year period, left UNESCO at the end of 1999. In that connection I recall when I was to receive best wishes on the occasion of my own retirement from the Paris headquarters staff in 1994. "You've done everything you wanted," Mayor told me as he shook my hand with a rascally smile. "And I didn't stop you!"

We have remained friends and will continue so for life.

After not meeting for a lapse of years, there arose a chance in the summer of 1998 for the two of us to chat. As he spoke to me of "A Culture of Peace," I suddenly realized that he was revisiting a seminal idea at the base of UNESCO's creation. Everything he had done from the moment he swept on that stage holding a small book in his hand had been consistent with this vision.

His ideas were always turned toward the future. "The past is already written. It cannot be changed. The only thing about it that can be changed is *décrier*, that is, how to describe it. However, we can write the future."

"To write the future" – now that is a wonderfully poetic expression.

At the time of my retirement, when I left his sixth-floor headquarters room in the secretariat, there were hanging in the corridor outside his office many pictures and posters from projects in which I had had a hand. I was stopped in my tracks in front of one of these, "The Road." It is a memorable work by the artist Kaii Higashiyama; it pictures a road climbing straight up a hill with no figure in sight. This masterpiece was never sold or given away during the artist's lifetime.

I remember, at the time of his leaving his post, I stood there and handed Frederico Mayor a lithograph of this art poster. "This road is the future," he said as he gazed at it intently. "Behind us lie heap upon heap of victims of exploitation and violence. This picture calls us to fill the road to this future with flowers."

Bridge 12

In this Encounter the reader glimpses a bit of the ongoing international controversy interwoven with the history of UNESCO. As mentioned earlier, both the governments of the United States and the United Kingdom quit UNESCO over financial and other concerns. Some critics of UNESCO have made unfavorable comparisons of UNESCO and UNICEF. We'll return to this issue in Encounter 34, "UNESCO for the World."

I would underline here that Hattori sees Mayor as a person who focuses our attention on the future. It is a future than can be strewn with flowers for children – indeed for all people and even for the natural environment itself. Leaders and philanthropists in both the private and public sectors are positioned to *see* dynamic linkages and actionable possibilities instead of just perplexing single issues or daunting obstacles. Such vision can indeed become world-transforming. Illustrative of the stature of Mayor is his complex relationship with the Spanish government.

Mayor came from the province of Catalonia, which was similar to Basque country in Spain. The Basques and Catalans were people of supreme confidence in their own cultures. This helps explain the failure of the Spanish government to recommend Mayor for his UNESCO position. However, the problem disappeared when Mayor later became quite close to King Carlos of Spain.

As for the artistic genius Kaii Higashiyama, Betty Rogers Rubenstein exposes the reasons for his fame. In 1987 Rubenstein characterized him as "Japan's most celebrated artist" and stated that his worldwide reputation extended "from Germany to China, from Rome to Washington." She attributes this reputation for his work to "his quiet but compelling landscapes and seascapes." Later in her essay she writes, "His well-known Flowers Luminous at Night exemplifies the poetic energy of his conceptions, which capture the mutability and rhythmic endurance of the natural world and the transformation of the art of seeing into an act of reverence." Hattori wholeheartedly approves of this assessment. As we have seen above, he felt it was indeed appropriate for Mayor to choose a work of Higashiyama's to help UNESCO and a world audience to see hope for the future.[2]

---

2. "Flowers of the Moon: the Art of Kaii Higashiyama" in the copyrighted feature "The World & I Online" at worldandi.com. The public portion of Rubenstein's article was accessed on 02/01/2004. The issue date of the article was April, 1987.

Part II
Words That Are Ensouled

Japan in the World
and
"Wisdom of the East"

13

Japan
A Country with "Soul-Filled" Words

Shinto is a "feeling" born of the soul and power of language in Japan. It can be reduced to three elements. They are peace, purification, and regeneration or rebirth.

"常世の重波寄する美し." This short quotation from classical Japanese literature roughly means, "Japan is a beautiful country that is constantly receiving waves on waves from distant lands of a sacred paradise."

In ancient times, according to the 8th-century "Chronicles of Japan" (*Nihonshoki*), the ensouled language that was inspired by the divine spirit was the language used when the goddess Yamato Hime no Mikoto transported the goddess Amaterasu to what is now the area of Ise.

The peoples living on the earth at about this time who revered the sun are too numerous to mention. Examples are found in Egypt, Persia, and the Inca Empire. Also, in Wakoku or Yamato (two names for ancient Japan), "Hinomiko" (a sun goddess) in due time fused the nation and the goddess Amaterasu Ōmikami into a single entity.[1] "*Hi*" (pronounced "he") not only means sun or fire but is also

---

1. Hattori's shocking enterprise is to lead every one of his readers from the very symbol many in the West associate with a nationalistic and militaristic expansionism to the Sun as the rather universal symbol of benign divinity. He even trumps that with his vision of Japan, his country of birth, as a wonderful example of a fusion of cultures

> # Ensouling?!
>
> Endowing with spirit, soul, essence or distinctive characteristics
>
> "Ensouling" is an unusual word, but the kind of endowment suggested by it here is even more unusual. I have chosen to use this weird word to alert the reader to the alien, shocking excursion that Hattori is leading us on in this Encounter.
>
> The strangeness may be mitigated if the reader realizes that, whether Hattori is endowing a language or a culture with a defining characteristic or "soul," all such souls complement each other to constitute humanity. Also, the defining lines between cultures are sometimes permeable, not razor sharp. Therefore, two cultures may overlap and share the same characteristic – say, esthetic creativity – though each does so in its distinctive manner. . . .

thought to mean soul or spirit. According to an ancient text, the founder of the Japanese imperial dynasty was Amaterasu Ōmikami, the Sun Goddess. . . .

The successive waves of incoming cultures are named Jōmon, Yayoi, and Yamato. Possibly the people of the Jōmon period (5th or 4th millennium B.C.-250 B.C.), may have been Ainu. They, along with the people who imported the Yayoi culture,[2] as well as the ones who created the Yamato Dynasty (300-710) came from a variety of places, and, after crossing oceans from North, South, and West, arrived at this chain of islands from overseas. The ancient saying quoted above refers to *tokuyo*, paradise, and may allude to the "home countries" or "birthplaces" from which waves of different peoples and cultures were brought one after another.

The Japan of ancient times was not a country of just one race. Furthermore, if homogeneity has characterized the Japanese people consistently, wouldn't that fact still be visible in those born today? (Persons outside Japan who assume that all Japanese look alike need to look more carefully.)

Among other National Treasures in the Kono Shrine, is found the "Genealogy of an ocean clan." According to it, Amabe, the chief priest mentioned, was of the 82nd generation of priests at that shrine; he set forth his thoughts in a short composition entitled, "The Soul of the Great Japanese Race":

> . . . . From the first, the Japanese people were not a single race. They were of many races and countries. In other words, I think that the Japanese islands in the Yōran period of history constituted a melting pot of ancient international

---

and races derived by the Sun's divine fiat from the many lands Sun passes over. This uses the traditions underlying jingoistic rhetoric to undermine and explode any presumptions on the part of his fellow citizens of a racial "purity" or "superiority" of culture uncontaminated by the outside barbarians.

2. The Yayoi time period is quite comparable to the Hellenistic period in the West (300 B.C.-300 A.D.)

cultures. Thus the advanced cultures and skills of the visitors and immigrants who came were completely melded and assimilated in the crucible provided by the Japanese islands. Furthermore, having received the very breath of the earth's soul as related to the strange and mysterious soul of Yamato, there occurred something like a rebirth of Yamato culture through the purifying stimulus from these outside influences.

The idea at which the priest Amabe is here hinting is *kotodama*, "the ensouled language of Yamato."

The study of many foreign languages shows me that whenever I grasp the meaning of something in a particular language, I have in a flash touched the very "soul" of that language; this seems to be the point that the priest Amabe is hinting at. In both French and German there are "ensouled words." If this is so, what kind of distinctive power or "soul" infuses Japanese words?[3]

The coexistence of many different peoples in this relatively small country was what functioned as the single dominant principle (or "soul") in ancient Japan, and it was the catalyst for the emergence of Yamato's language, which is what is becoming known as *kotodama*. Japan at that time had not so much "reason," logic, or Logos (Greek and Western) as the benefit of their unique language. It is a language that conveys or evokes the thing-itself. In other words, the Japanese language became *pathos*, that is, the direct and plain expression of whatever was deeply felt.[4]

The language of Yamato, as found in some of the earliest Japanese literature, possesses limitless lucidity and serenity. The purifying astonishment it evokes invites me into a transparent world that may be described as *seimeishin*, that is, the world of "the bright and clear heart." Perhaps in the artless simplicity of its language, the world of *Manyōshū*[5] falls short of the later more developed spirituality of Japanese literature. The formation of such spirituality had to await the kind of thinking associated with Zen and Pure Land Buddhism as they flourished in discussions during the Kamakura Period (12th-14th centuries). However, in this earlier language of the *Manyōshū* there is a rhythm that plays wonderfully upon the ears in what seems to gush forth from the earth of Japan so as to keep the land richly verdant. The language has put down a wide root system. Even when Chinese words were imported into the Japanese language[6]

---

3. Some of Hattori's ideas here are explored further in my short article, "An Introduction to the Thought of Global Thinker Eiji Hattori: Ensouled Language and the Sound of Snow," in *Asian Profile* (Vol. 33, No. 6, December, 2005), 547-554. The approach seeks to integrate philosophic, literary, and religious perspectives.
4. The word παθος (pathos) in classical Greek refers to the emotion conveyed by effective speech or drama. "Empathy" in modern English is a closely related word and concept.
5. Poetry anthology completed in the eighth century.
6. *Kanbun* is the word for this; it means the Chinese writing system used to express the Chinese classics in Japanese.

there is something that suggests just how deeply rooted in the Japanese culture this *Yamato kotoba* ("ancient Japanese") was. Thus it can be said that "Japanese" people are the people who built up their culture with the fundamental *sounds* of the old Yamato language so that the "Japanese soul" is virtually their *breath of life* as well as their heart and mind.

Once while the philosopher Ari Mori was giving a lecture in Paris, he firmly answered the question of who the Japanese are by saying, "They are the ones who speak Japanese."

While people were astonished by Mori's extremely simple definition, his concept was born of insight based on much reflection. This philosopher, as a result of devoting himself completely to understanding the meaning and mystery of language, was able to see the formation of the Japanese people by the "soul" found in the language of Yamato. That soul or spirit is still running in the lifeblood of the Japanese language up to this very day. The fact is that from early times the Japanese people were shaped by *kotodama* as embodied in the language of Yamato.

Bridge 13

The Japanese contribution in the moral sphere has been considerable. Hattori imprints the reality:

> Shinto is a deep feeling or sympathy born out of the "ensouled" Japanese language. It can be reduced to three elements. They are peace, purification, and regeneration or rebirth. "Peace" is the heart and soul of Yamato, and in the constitution issued in 604 AD by Prince Shotoku (the imperial sponsor of Buddhism in Japan), we find the words: "Harmony is to be valued." "Purification" is the restoration to purity by the washing away of the past by means of fire, water, and salt. These are items that, according to Mircea Eliade, are bound together in an archetype of the world's religions as the "eternal return." The third element, *saisei* (rebirth or revitalization), is what is symbolized by the priests' removal and rebuilding of a shrine. Whether it's a shrine, a house, or a human being, the principle is the same. At certain times through a ceremony of purification something is reborn or reincarnated as a new existence. What best symbolizes this is seen in the events associated with the celebration of the New Year.

Historian Sidney Brown elaborates helpfully on the matter with which Hattori and I deal on the first page of this chapter on Japanese religious and mythic traditions:

> Former Prime Minister Abe Shinzo sought to revive nationalism by visiting the Yasukuni Shrine, and by amending the constitution to allow unfettered

development of military forces. His approach failed to interest the Japanese voters, but this work [*Deep Encounters*] might be considered to be in line with the Abe approach unless the purpose is clearly explained.

Our page one, including the footnote and my boxed comment, is this book's way of indicating the distance between our work and Prime Minister Abe's approach. To the above Brown adds an appropriate conclusion.

> The notion that the Japanese people are a product of the melting pot, based on a diversity of peoples who migrated to the islands, is an important one. Ethnicity not race is the fundamental distinction of peoples. The Japanese "are the ones who speak Japanese." (Letter dated October 28, 2007)

14

What Is the Form of Japan?
Concerning the Feminine Principle

There is a new feminine principle. According to it, reason resonates with sensitivity. I suspect that this is a very important message for the world, one that has arisen in Asia.

One morning, in a dream at daybreak when I was a little past my 20th birthday, I beheld an image of Japan.

It was a woman standing quite still on top of a hill. She was garbed in white clothing. The place where she stood was surrounded by a luminous atmosphere tinted silver gray. Her lips were touched with a faint smile.

I was not able to explain how the shape of Japan could be similar to this scene from an early-morning dream. However, it was something engraved into my heart as definitely true. I did share the experience with the fellow-student with whom I was lodging.

This vision never recurred and seemed on the point of dying away into oblivion. But about twenty years later, my experience as a young man came again to mind in a shocking way. This happened when André Malraux, as French Minister of Culture, visited Japan. Queried by a press group about his impression of Japan, he answered simply, "*Légèrement le jour*" (a faint dawn).

Wasn't that the ambiance for what I had seen twenty years earlier – a white-robed woman standing on a hill wrapped in dawn's light? During his brief stay in Japan, this man of letters, with his polished sensitivity, looked around Japan directing an intense gaze on all he experienced and thereby hit exactly upon the country's essence. He saw the same light that had illumined my vision.

The incident with Malraux astonished me and gave me an opportunity to reflect even more deeply on the day when I had that strange vision. It was during that youthful period that I got involved with existential philosophy while still in Japan. I can especially recall being somewhat under the spell of Kierkegaard as an aloof figure who grimly confronts God. Imitation of that figure led me to such extremes that I wandered about in the darkness of night or climbed alone from a misty mountain valley to a peak; in such ways I expressed my proud independence. As a student of Western philosophy, my state of mind became one in which hope and despair coexisted as though on a single page. I experienced in Kierkegaard the outermost limit in individualistic spirituality. Perhaps it was in this personal situation that I glimpsed an image of Japan that stood at the opposite extremity from Kierkegaard. When I look back on it all, I feel I understood, though vaguely, the experiences I was having in those early days.

There exists in some countries and cultures a "world" where pairs of principles sharply contend with each other. Examples of such opposites are the logical and illogical, the spiritual and the physical, the objective and subjective, not to mention moral scruples vs. the largely amoral claims of "rationality." Instead of continuing these unproductive debates, we perhaps need to think of them as appropriate only in a world dominated by the "masculine" where somebody has to win, and somebody else has to lose. Such a world requires correction by a complementary "feminine" principle. In Japan – particularly in traditional Japan – many thoughtful people could gently embrace what are considered in other times and places to be polar opposites.

About twenty years ago I encountered the saying, "A feminine principle was at work in the creation of Japan." The words had been spoken by the famous novelist Ryōtarō Shiba (1923-1996) in a dialogue with the distinguished American authority on Japan, Donald Keene. Shiba identifies the archetype for original Japanese culture with *taoyameburi*, the "way of a graceful maiden." He compares this with *masuraoburi*, the "way of manliness."[1] Historical circumstances including contacts with foreign countries sometimes elevated the literature of masculinity, *masuraoburi*, but the mainstream of Japanese literature had, since its very origin, always been based on *taoyameburi*, the feminine principle.

The masculine principle described here is *universal and objective*. Opposed to that is a way that is *personal and subjective*. In the "way of the man," the subject seeking the objective view is independent of the object, while in the "way of the woman," the observer becomes somehow united with the object. Because of its women writers, the culture of the Heian Period superbly exemplified the

---

1. Poems in ancient Japan were written by both men and women. The ones by women sounded feminine and the ones by men, masculine. Hence, the expressions "way of the woman" and "way of the man" arose.

feminine principle, but the manifestation of that principle was not limited to such 11th-century examples as Lady Murasaki Shikibu or Sei Shōnagon. The tradition of the feminine principle shows itself in literary collections extending from the ancient times reflected in the *Kōkin-shū*[2] to such examples in the Meiji Era as Masaoka Shiki, a male poet. According to Motoori Norinaga (1730-1801), the culture of *aware* (pathos or sensitive compassion) has produced a genre of culture that is almost never seen in foreign countries. The Japanese people are fond of Chinese poems. However, they specifically prefer a *Shi-shōsetsu* poet like Haku Rakuten,[3] who emphasizes the affectionate heart. This Japanese mentality of *aware* produced the genre of the "I-novel" (*shi-shōsetsu*), which is not commonly seen in foreign countries. "Femininity," which is perhaps better spoken of as "the feminine principle," should never imply self-deprecation or subservience – rather, just the opposite.

Modern world history, beginning with the 17th century, may be said to be the history of a mindset that rules things by dividing them and breaking them in pieces; such dissection re-creates the world artificially and, in the end, destroys it. Rationalism, the principle that assumes reason's supremacy in all ways, was engendered by the dominance of the *male principle*, and it was from this that there came about an alienation from being human in the integrated sense of humble *sainthood*. Saints possess both sensitivity and spirituality; they even glow with divinity, as we sense in St. Francis of Assisi.

Scientism is the offspring of a "masculine" or macho way of thinking that disregards or denigrates saintliness. In regard to such polarities as East and West, it tends to think that if West does not subdue East (or the South), then the West will be subdued or be destroyed itself. Such reasoning saturates highly militarized nations even among Western countries; it has, in my opinion, eventually contributed to colonialism and two world wars. At last it has brought us to the brink of destroying the earthly environment that is humanity's only habitat.

Professor Hayao Kawai has also emphasized that we must think again about the feminine principle now that the survival of humanity in the 21st century has become an acute problem. That is a very important message for the world, one that had its origin in Asia and yet is everywhere applicable.

However, before we Japanese send out such a message, we need to reflect deeply on what we lost in the prosperity of material civilization. This was during

---

2. A 10th-century compilation of old poems.
3. Haku Rakuten (also written, Hakurakuten) is the name of a Chinese poet famous in Japan. His name in Chinese is Po Chü-I, and he lived 772-847. The dramatist Seami wrote a Noh play about Haku Rakuten's visiting Japan for a contest with Japanese poets. In the conclusion, as a result of a dance of gods, a wind blows Po Chü-i's ship back to China. Po Chü-i's significance for Japan and the world is not so easily banished, because his poetry replaced the stiffness of a courtly style with simpler language and a deeper concern for social justice and moral well-being.

the time when Japan, having appropriated 19th-century Western scientism under the rallying cry of "Western science and Japanese spirit," still had not yet lost sight of the danger hiding in the shadow of "civilized prosperity." The same situation occurred in all the Southeast Asian countries that followed the lead of Japan for about fifty years.

Comparisons of the East and West must be made very carefully. Careless comparisons produce only argumentative and contentious results. If one is to make distinctions, it is best to start with the difference between the worlds *before* and *after* the Western scientific revolution of the 17th century. The Celtic culture of ancient Europe was very similar to that of some the early dwellers in the Japanese archipelago, that is, the people of the Jōmon period in Japan.[4] At the present time, some minority peoples of the earth transmit the early and original heritages of humanity. Indians of the Amazon and the Ainu of Japan share a common *kokoro* (heart/mind).

However, we cannot return to the Middle Ages, much less more ancient times. Goods produced by scientific technology must be clearly recognized as distinctive. But, in addition, we must consider what an overemphasis on cognitive training takes away, and return to a harmony of intellect, feeling and will.

There should be a new feminine principle. According to it, we must let reason resonate with sensitivity.

Bridge 14

One usage of English distinguishes "house" from "home." Humanity is wrecking house and home. (Wasn't "housing" provided by Mother Nature and "home" by Father God?) It is all too apparent that the human family is in danger of tearing house and home apart. A proverb tells us it takes love to make one's house a home. The *feminine principle* invites us to use our time well to become a human family. It would be easy to give up on the present assemblage of quarreling brats.

In my darker moments a "Little Gray Devil" torments me. His most recent taunt runs, "How can you and Hattori be so complacent about 'the feminine principle' when you, Wallace, know from the morning news that it's baloney? Don't tell me you don't remember the mother who has always 'loved' her son by smoking marijuana in front of the 6-year-old and later by cooking methamphetamine with him. She shed sentimental tears over his death sentence for shooting and killing his sheriff while high on meth. So?"

---

4. Technically Jōmon refers to a major early culture of Japan extending from around 10,000 to 300 BC (with the peak coming around 5,000 BC). It was characterized by distinctive dwellings and pottery.

I have no definitive answer to that, but Confucius with his doctrine of the rectification of names may provide a partial answer: "Father" no longer means father; "Mother" no longer means mother. We need to "rectify" names by using these words in terms of right behavior and not merely in terms of biology or gross distortions of parenting.

15

Freedom and Nature
Learning from Daisetsu Suzuki

> If nature in the sense of the Japanese word *jinen* (and Spinoza's *natura*) includes the possibility of uniting the self with the order of nature as its laws permeate the universe, that fact suggests what real freedom is.

In 1998, after a year of Japanese anticipation, the "Statue of Liberty" from France began to command the view of Tokyo Bay. It was transported all the way from Paris in connection with a "France Year" in Japan, which was held in response to the "Japan Year" that was celebrated in France the previous year.

In 1876 the French government presented the U.S. with the Statue of Liberty to celebrate the 100th anniversary of the founding of the United States of America. In return for that gift, in 1889 the American Club of Paris[1] presented Paris with a small replica of the very same Liberty statue. The statue built on Swan Island on a sandbar in the Seine faces across the Atlantic toward the Statue of Liberty in New York Harbor. The word "Liberty" in the statue's name is part of the motto of the

---

1. In connection with the closing days of the American Revolution, Benjamin Franklin founded the American Club of Paris, now the oldest non-diplomatic club of its kind. Its membership evolved from an American one to a Franco-American blend, and eventually to multi-national inclusiveness. Today younger members are being recruited, and one-third of the members are women. For more information visit http://www.americanclubparis.org

French Revolution so familiar to everyone: "Liberty, Equality, Fraternity." From the embodiment of that word in a statue has arisen a benefit that accrues to all nations, a message with contemporary value that flies beyond Franco-American friendship. Throughout the world freedom is loudly advocated and widely sought. Of course, that is good. However, how many people are aware of the weight and seriousness of the word? To begin with, is the word or the Western understanding of the word universal, i.e., found in the same form in every nation? No, for the word *jiyū* (actually meaning self-dependent) was used by Nishi Amane in the early part of the Meiji era in the 19th century to translate the occurrence of words for liberty in European and American books. *Liberté* and *Freiheit* were the French and German words.

Amane is the man who coined the Japanese words for "philosophy" (*tetsugaku*) and "logic" (*ronri*), etc., and each of his excellent translations had its own delicacy and charm. These new words, which were the product of novel combinations of Chinese characters, were re-exported to China. It should be noted that until the neologism *jiyū* was created, there was no such word in Japanese or Chinese. In fact, all words designate their respective realities, physical or conceptual. For example, the Japanese word *tokonoma* does not exist outside the Japanese language except as a strange-sounding word in large dictionaries. That's because the *tokonoma* in its sense of a distinctive kind of alcove in Japanese architecture does not exist outside Japan.

When I was a student, it worried me that such an important idea as freedom would have to be imported into the Japanese language. There should be something else. It was Suzuki Daisetsu[2] (already famous for explaining Zen in fluent English in Europe and America) who answered this question for me and thereby opened my eyes to a fresh approach to the issue of what freedom is. I felt illuminated listening to his lecture on Japanese spirituality at Kyoto University. After the many richly suggestive comments he made on "the transfiguration in Confucianism of *jin* (benevolence and humanity) into *gi* (justice)," he said, "In Japan the word that best corresponds to 'freedom' must be *jinen* (naturing)." (I interpret this as what Spinoza referred to in using the present participle in his famous Latin expression *natura naturans*.)

This word is often used in the verbal expression *jinen suru* (which literally translates into the highly unusual English verb "natures," a neologism formed

---

2. More commonly referred to in the West as D. T. Suzuki. (This may have been Suzuki's choice for presenting his name to readers of English.) To my knowledge the Japanese do not use anything comparable to initials, nor do they have middle names. Professor Hattori chooses here the formal way of listing the name in Japanese style as befitting a deceased and highly respected scholar and sensei. Later in the chapter "Old Master" again reflects the respect-language accorded a person of Suzuki's stature and renown.

from the noun "nature"),³ but Suzuki's announcement became the key that opened a door in my thinking. Where in the structure of consciousness does the distinction between freedom and nature lie? Here's what I discovered:

The concept of freedom that arose in the West refers to freedom *from something or other*. The prototype for that kind of freedom resides in the relation between master and slave. The moment when a slave is liberated is freedom. Freedom in the modern world means *release from exploitation*. An existentialist philosopher may be concerned with "freedom from God." Sartre as an heir of Nietzsche's declaration, "God is dead," was looking for *the way to freedom* in this sense. He depicted human existence as something arising when the perfect freedom of the deceased God is bestowed on human beings. The person faced with boundless nothingness feels disoriented and nauseous. So, it was not something thoughtlessly simple like "egoism" or "pleasing yourself," but, instead, it concerned a way of strict and difficult decision-making by the individual as the self's one and only lord.

We must notice that such radically individualistic decision-making always carries with it the danger of self-destruction. Why? Because in this essential structure of "being free from something" (in the sense of an *outside* constraint) the self creates in itself something constraining and then tries to escape from this new constraint. It is in such a moment that an abyss appears in one's mind.

"When I look down into the abyss, the abyss looks back at me." These are the words of a 14-year-old Kobe youngster referred to only as "A" at the time of the discovery of his incredible murder of an 11-year-old child in 1997.⁴ The quotation comes from his composition entitled, "The Madness of Absolute Nothingness."

On this point of dangerous self-conflict, recent developments in immunology give us a great hint. The renowned immunologist Tomio Tada describes a highly dangerous condition in the immune system known as autoimmune disorder, in which the immune system attacks its own body's tissues. The parallel to the tragic case of "A" is that his horrific crime sprang both from outside influences and from an internal disorder similar to autoimmune disorders. That is, *we need others* for our own subsistence.

The freedom that was born in the West is, to the bitter end, a *freedom of opposing and fighting against* . . . . In contrast to this stands what Suzuki Daisetsu

---

3. Suzuki's usage seems mainly to betoken the kind of freedom exhibited by selves that are not at odds with themselves or the world of nature. In positive terms we may extend this concept of freedom to suggest that nature at its best provides the brain power to cure or relieve nature's own defects, such as cancer. The same brains should be capable of correcting human nature's propensities toward destructive conflict, perhaps by finding or perfecting workable means of peace. This does not preclude use of ways of peace advocated by the spiritual and religious traditions of mankind.
4. The crime to which Hattori refers was a grisly act of decapitation much publicized and discussed at the time in Japan and abroad.

says about *nature*. Nature is *just as it is* – not fighting either external or self-imposed restraints – but in harmony with itself. So, being perfectly free means to function at one with the laws of nature. The Old Master has taught us that perfect freedom is born from a fusion with nature. Let us consider an example as close at hand as our own bodies.

People dread water, people drown in water, and yet dolphins swim in water, and there are people who play in it. How should we account for this difference? The "dreaders" or "drowners" do not yet know water. The swimmers master water by uniting with its laws and principles. If the expression *natura naturans* designates a unification with the orderliness of nature that fills the whole universe, "nature" in that sense should be an authentic kind of freedom, should it not?

Bridge 15

In the Note to his Japanese readers, Hattori reiterates that "winning freedom" in the West refers to fighting against something and for something else. A dramatic example of this is seen in Delacroix's most famous painting from 1830, "Liberty Leading the People" (now housed in the Louvre). Here the Goddess of Liberty stands in the swirling smoke of battle among armed defenders. She has a flag in her raised right hand and a bayoneted rifle in her left. Hattori sharply contrasts this with one major Eastern perspective.

> The point of view is "white cloud and running water" as spoken of in Zen. In other words it's the way nature is as it is, and functions as it functions. Whenever that state is reached, the state of original freedom has been won. Also, to go toward that state is the purpose of mental, physical, and spiritual training.
>
> There is law in everything. For example, anyone will fall down when first learning to ride a bicycle, but when one masters the dynamics of the bike as a moving body, there arises a way of riding it with smooth and quiet freedom. . . . In contrast, when the laws of nature are not known, every aspect of human existence is unfree.

In correspondence, Hattori has elaborated:

> "Freedom from oppression" presupposes that leaders should manifest virtue, not power. In ancient China this was a requirement of anyone becoming emperor, and when violated, it became a reason for the change of dynasties.

* * *

From my end of the bridge, it seems appropriate here to quote and comment on a sentence with which Hattori concluded his note to Japanese readers: "I still remember well what I received from the lecture of Master Suzuki fifty years ago. It opened my understanding to this 'wisdom of the East.'"

In the exclusive sense, "Wisdom of the East" is ethnocentric nonsense; the term has been used in ways that Hattori and I consider a mind-trap. The East has no patent on wisdom; the West has produced its sages whom Hattori and many other scholars have utilized and discussed in some detail. Also, when we carefully search, we discover in both the East and West ancient origins of science and its metaphysically modern implications. *Certainly there are significant expressions of mysticism, art, and democracy east, west, north and south*, but, in important particulars, all these vary from region to region and turn out to be worthily complementary rather than mutually exclusive.

* * *

Davion: As a football player I'm tempted to fall like a piece of glass and end up broken. Training helps me use my natural flexibility. So, if I go limp like a rag, I'll get up in one piece free from injury to body or pride. This is the way I interpret Suzuki as explained by Professor Hattori. It's a wise and very freeing way.

16

The Hidden Being
Monotheism and Polytheism

In their inmost thinking the Japanese realize that the gods take various shapes, the Buddhas as well being fleeting images; also there's the awareness of the transitory nature of these apparent beings. Through these various shapes, the Japanese can see the One, the "Life-Source" or perhaps the "Hidden God."

> I don't know what is[1] there
> But, struck with gratitude, my eyes overflow with tears

This poem in tanka-style,[2] composed by the 11th-century Buddhist priest Saigyō-hōshi, is said to have been written at the Ise Shrine. Its words will not leave my mind, though its meaning has only dawned on me by degrees. The poem seems saturated by Japanese feeling. Saigyō as a Buddhist priest was prohibited from entering the grounds of the Shrine. He must, therefore, have looked at the

---

1. Hattori informs me that the verb *owashimasu* is reserved for a divine being. When an ordinary person is being referred to, "to be" = *imasu*," but when a divine being is implicit, *owashimasu* is the more formal or higher-toned verb. This fact of language justifies an alternative interpretation of the poem:
   > I don't know what divinity deigns to be there
   > But, struck with gratitude, my eyes overflow with tears
2. Poems of the *tanka* form are a distinctive category of Japanese literature. They contain short units named *haiku* (incorporating three lines in a syllabic pattern of 5-7-5) that are more famous outside Japan than the fuller antecedent form.

Inner Shrine of Ise from across the river Isuzu. The strong and deep feelings that affected him show the bottomless mystery of the purified space that characterizes Ise.

A world of syncretism where gods and Buddhas are reconciled, as is the case in Japan, is one full of myriads of Shinto gods and goddesses and numerous Buddhas and Bodhisattvas. In religious studies, such a world is presumed to be polytheistic. Besides, in Hegel's dialectical view of history, polytheism is a form of religion that succeeds animism globally. It is suited to societies of ancient times and hence, Hegel thinks, appears in uncivilized societies where it emerges as a superior form of religion to be displaced at a later stage in the more advanced societies by Christian monotheism.

However, is the *kami*[3] that dwells in Japanese hearts really plural? This question has recurred to my mind off and on for some time. One day, while the question continued to nag at my mind, I happened upon an answer.

If we paraphrase the idea that God as the ultimate god is "hidden being," we may say:

The universal God as One is invisible. But that One exists.

From primitive times humanity everywhere has come to experience the existence of a great spirit that arouses awe. What is called *mana* in the South Pacific and *numen* in the West has been expressed by Rudolf Otto as *das Heilige* (the Holy or numenal). This holy divinity does not immediately become the Creator. It exists along with nature. It is not the creator of heaven and earth. It exists within the fountainhead of heaven and earth. And it is what arrives in the "here and now" as the great river of life. It is not a transcendent deity. There is no gap between the supreme God and humanity. All gods who appear in the *Kojiki* and the *Nihonshoki*[4] are transformations of the "hidden self" of God into our mortal bodily existence. In other words, they are manifestations in the human world of One who is universal. From those early times, that One had all kinds of names and human personalities. The Hidden One in these various manifestations acted as human beings do. Even the Buddha also appeared in all sorts of forms. However, to the Japanese mind, at least unconsciously, they are all phenomena (apparitions, forms), metamorphoses of the fundamental One, the Life-Source. When I consider this point carefully, it appears to me that it is going to resolve many questions and doubts.

Why do Japanese have both an altar for the Shinto gods as well as a Buddhist altar? Why are they going to visit a shrine or temple without knowing the name of the tutelary deity? In visiting a temple, why does it make any difference whether its principal image is that of Dainichi Buddha, Amida Buddha, or Kannon?

---

3. *Kami*, like other Japanese nouns, can be interpreted as either singular or plural.
4. "Records of Ancient Matters" and "Chronicles of Japan." These early 8th-century documents are comparable in some ways to Homer's *Iliad* and *The Odyssey*.

Dainichi in Japan is Mahavairocana in India; Kannon is Avalokitesvara there. Both are from Esoteric Buddhism. Amida, i.e. Amitaba, has no esoteric character. Amida belongs to the faith of Pure Land introduced to Japan from China at the end of the Heian Period (12th century). Moreover, there are deities such as Benzai-Ten (Sarasvati) or Taishaku-Ten (Indra) who belong to Hinduism.

However, without discriminating among all these, the Japanese seem to be placing their hands reverently together in front of each of them. In fact, they do not question the meaning of these Buddhas. Is that from mere ignorance?

From the American or European point of view, it's at least very strange. But I do not think it strange. What the Japanese feel deeply, even if unconsciously, is expressed in the saying, "Even Buddhas are nothing but dust."

In other words, the gods and Buddhas who appear in many forms are, after all, phenomena or somewhat perceivable presences whom we encounter in our mortal lives. They all are like a cloud of dust through which we can intuit the Source of Life. Whenever our existence, on occasion, is illuminated, the "Hidden God" may then become imperfectly manifest. This somewhat modest approach allows Japanese to pray in a Christian church. Generally speaking, Christian believers seem to feel they should not pray in a Buddhist temple.

Let us review the formative stages of Judaism where monotheism came to be firmly established. According to Exodus, Moses (13th century B.C.), having led the Jewish people to cross the Red Sea and thus escape from Egypt, concludes a covenant with Yahweh (Jehovah). In the Ten Commandments, which he received from God, we find the words, "You shall believe in no gods besides me." (Exodus 20:3)

The Koranic phrase, "There is no god but Allah," is based on these words as much as is Judaism, but to me the wording seems somewhat strange. The reason is that unless the people assumed there were other gods, such words would be unnecessary. In fact, in Egypt, which was fundamentally polytheistic about the time of Moses, Baal, a god that had been carried in by the Phoenicians, was very popular. It was a Baal with the head of a calf. In this historical context the word for religion (*religio* in Latin) carries the meaning of "binding" or "linking up with someone." That implies a covenant made by a certain people with a certain god, whereupon that

---

**Tolerant Reverence
or
Polite Indifference?**

When today's Japanese visit some sacred site and reverently place their hands together in a temple, clap at a shrine, or bow in a church, are they merely being polite? They may be displaying some of the positive attitudes or deep intuitions attributed to them by Hattori. They may instead be mildly apathetic, harboring entirely secular thoughts. At heart they may even be antagonistic toward all religious "superstitions." Hattori feels this is too strong.

We do agree that people have depths that mere observation cannot always probe. – WG

people becomes a "chosen people."

So this genealogy of monotheism is surprisingly polytheistic. Some recent scholars refer to a "monotheizing tendency" in ancient Israel to distinguish this phase from a more fully formed monotheism.

That is the primary significance of Christ's dying on a cross. True and full monotheism is not for *a chosen people* but for the *whole of humanity*. To receive that disclosure, we had to wait for Jesus Christ.

Bridge 16

The full impact of what Hattori is saying is found in his concluding paragraph in the main text of this chapter. Realizing as most Jewish and Christian scholars do, that there are universalistic passages in the Old Testament, he nevertheless holds to the conviction that both the Cross and some of Jesus' parables climactically broaden the category of those deserving compassion as well as capable of offering it. The really *good* Samaritan was purposely *chosen* by Jesus from a traditionally despised outside group to make his point about the truly good neighbor. The Samaritans had been hated all the more, because, though monotheistic, they differed from Judaism even on what belonged in the sacred canon, i.e., only the five books of the Pentateuch out of a possible 39. (For the parable on the Good Samaritan consult Luke 10:25-37.) In his Note Hattori goes on to state:

Although a Jew himself, Jesus gives up the Chosen People way of looking at things. "What are we to make

---

Light of the World
As the
Firefly Winks

By the Reverend Dr. Dale Robison
American Historian and Unitarian Minister

The meeting of philosopher Wallace Gray and Japanese scholar Eiji Hattori expresses how the many encounters of life – of persons, places and things – may seem at times, to be no more than "Winking Fireflies." Seen along hedges their light is ephemeral, as insignificant as sparkling particles of dust. Captive in an empty fruit jar and held close, they light up palms and cheeks. Authentic human encounters and Divine-Human encounters may seem to be initially low-wattage and infrequent, but taken together they light up our lives and the universe.

"The light shines in the darkness and the darkness shall not overcome it." The opening of John's Gospel resonates with the life of Jesus as the light which shines forth from a Divine-Human encounter. Jewish theologian Martin Buber's *Ich-Du* (I-Thou) indicates that in authentic human encounter, infinity and universality – the divine – is actualized. On the far side of the world Hindus greet one another with *Namaste:* "I honor the place in you in which the entire Universe dwells. I honor the place in you which is of Love, or Peace and Light." The reciprocity of the greeting is a given.

of Jesus Christ?" Hattori asks. The emphatic answer is that Jesus' message is one in which we discover God *dwelling in the midst of all the people of the world.*

I well remember the striking words of a rabbi who recently spoke at our Protestant liberal-arts college. He made clear that he and his house (to echo Scripture) worshipped the God of Abraham, Isaac, and Jacob in the mode of his Jewish tradition while at the same time remaining respectful of the closest "outsider," the Jew Jesus – an outsider to Judaism and the rabbi because of claims made on his behalf, not so much on account of his own person or life.

The rabbi went further to explain that his own loyalty to the God of Abraham and Moses did not prevent him from appreciating traditions such as Shinto in which worshipping "other gods" seemed appropriate.

17

A Bird Calls, Then the Mountain Deepens Its Silence
Reflections in a Tea Pavilion

There is a place (*ba*) filled with "space-time." Everything is being born with, and as a companion to, human beings. That occurs wherever we realize that the existence of other things deeply affects the existence of self. In fact, the existence of all others gives authentication to, and evidence of, the "private" self.

I remember a particular morning in a place where the clean air itself seemed tinted green.[1] It was in the temple of Kōzan-ji[2] in the very northernmost area of Kyoto, an area isolated from the noise and clamor of cities. I was seated in the tea pavilion of this charming mountain temple where I was surrounded by a faint fragrance of incense, the gentle shushing sound made by the hot water on its charcoal brazier, and the elegant calligraphy displayed on a scroll in the tokonoma. In handwriting from the hand of a *rōshi* (an aged priest), the scroll displayed these words . . .

　　　　. . . birdcall, mountain calm . . .

鳥啼きて山さらに幽かなり

---

1. The Japanese *aoi* refers to blue, green, and blue-green.
2. A secluded temple northwest of Kyoto. Here the famous Zen founder Eisai brought the tea plant from China to monk Myo-e, who started a garden to produce tea. Tea may

The white-haired tea-master Hisamatsu Shin'ichi[3], widely known as a disciple of the philosopher Nishida Kitarō, is setting forth for us the procedures for the tea ceremony. This was after the period he spent as professor of religious studies at Kyoto University. On the present occasion, I am attending an integrative ceremony, a "tea ceremony of the mind" over which Master Hisamatsu presides. He suddenly stops, and turning his gentle face toward us, says, "It must be the bird referred to in the calligraphy."[4]

"When the mountain is filled with silence, the call of the bird will break the hush. With that call the silence is deepened."

If we view matters merely from the physical point of view, there is not supposed to be a deeper stillness than the complete absence of noise. However, Zen teaches that a silence is greatly intensified by the intervention of a single sound. That is a truth from a unique dimension never grasped by scientific rationalism; only spiritually can we learn from that truth. At such a time human beings breathe harmoniously with nature, perhaps even "inhaling" it.

My first encounter with the small group known as the "Society for Tea of the Mind" (kokoro = the heart/mind) was on the day of a matriculation ceremony. I suppose it might have occurred at any university, but, as it turned out, on the premises of Kyoto University I saw varicolored placards and paper banners lined up in a row advertising different clubs and circles in order to recruit as many students as possible. In a place far apart from the others, I noticed a piece of paper with a short announcement written by brush.

Needed: Ten New Members
of
Society for Tea-of-the-Mind

I decided to try to go to the interview place in the announced hall. The persons I found there reminded me of priests in a row, with faces that said, "We will never take an evil-minded man."

"Do you know anything about sadō?

"In high school I learned the Urasenke style of Tea."

"Have you read Professor Hisamatsu's book?"

"Yes, I was deeply impressed by his 'Mu^5 in the Orient.'"

"What point particularly impressed you?"

---

have been initially used to help meditating monks stay awake. Myo-e became deeply attracted by Kegon, a form of Japanese Buddhism that emphasizes the dependence of all phenomena upon each other.

3. Hōseki (1890-1980) is his Buddhist name.
4. Presumably, the Master heard this kind of song while helping his students enter the silence of Tea.
5. Nothingness in Zen's philosophical sense.

"The point that, for Zen, nothing is sacred."⁶

Several days later I was notified by postcard that my admission to Tea Ceremony of the Mind had been approved. The group's activity included pilgrimages to old temples. Monthly the *Kokoro* society was in the habit of touring a noted temple in Kyoto (the old capital). A meeting can be characterized as follows:

> To be accepted . . .
>
> To be accepted, what's required? No doubt the self-discipline of Hattori at times must have seemed like that of the legendary Chinese student who gathered enough fireflies in one place to enable him to study *all night*! In his Preface, Hattori, speaking in the French manner, alludes to such times as "white nights."

> At our pleasure now, we enter the hermitage's pure court,
> Participate in the profound meaning of *sadō*⁷,
> Thus learning the Law of WA-KEI-SEI-JAKU."⁸

The meeting begins with the chanting of this Maxim of the Way of Tea written by the master. The ceremony consists of three parts: *Zazen* (meditation), *Tea*, and the *Master's Discourse*.

We brush off the dust and trash of the mind by *sitting* in meditation one hour. After passing through the garden, which is now swept and purified, we then *cleanse* the hands and mouth with water and *enter* the tea room through its very small door. This enables us to empty the mind of all the daily burdens of work, status, age, etc., and enter a world of the "non-ordinary."

We would like to climb the fragrant path left by sages and saints . . . .

Sitting upright while linking our voices in chant, we concentrate our minds. Keeping firmly in mind the ultimate truth of the "beauty of forlorn sobriety"⁹ we concentrate on diligently awakening the heart and mind, seeing one's whole life in a single encounter, studying in the Zen manner the futility of good sense and propriety as well as the fact that one has lost interest in moral principles. . . . .

---

6. Hattori places this statement in its Zen context: *"Nothing is sacred" is equivalent to saying that everything is sacred. There is no transcendence, therefore no immanence.*
7. *Sadō* = Way of Tea.
8. WA-KEI-SEI-JAKU = Harmony-Respect-Purity-Serenity. It is interesting that JAKU, which originally meant serenity, evolved to mean loneliness! To a person lacking serenity, one who has that quality may seem lonesome – *too* alone.
9. This phrase is Hattori's English translation of *wabisuki*. In modern non-traditional non-technical Japanese *wabi* refers to a subdued taste, a taste for the simple and quiet. *Suki*, on the other hand, refers to artistic taste like that expressed in a refined art such as the Way of Tea.

At that time, like many others, I was passing through the springtime of my life with a lot of worries and troubles. In order to obtain stillness and serenity of mind, I practiced Zen at such temples as Daitokuji and Myōshinji. However, there was one big question that stood in front of me as a barrier to my understanding extreme or ultimate enlightenment. (The technical term for this in Zen is *kensho*, a combination of characters meaning to *see* or *wake up* to the Truth; the second character is the one still in general use for Enlightenment. As a stand-alone word, it is read *satori*. But when combined with *ken* it connotes extreme, perhaps perfect satori.)

My sticky question was, *Why is satori necessary?* I flung this question at Professor Nishitani,[10] and it troubled him. In more personal form, my question may be stated, "What on earth is the meaning of salvation for me as a lone self, individual, or ego?"

It was at a time like this that the Tea Circle of the Mind opened up for me the fuller meaning for "Enlightenment" or satori. It was the insight that *space-time is fulfilled*. Such a time is born when you are "with another person."

Wabicha (abstemious tea) is a term utitlized by Rikyū, who drastically modified Sadō (*Way of Tea*).[11] There is a time when space-time is fulfilled. Such a time is born when you are "with another person." Everything is being born along with, and as a companion to, human beings. Accordingly, the existence of other persons deeply touches and benefits the existence of self. In fact, the existence of others gives authentication to, and evidence of, "my" self.[12] (In a more general sense, the preceding topics may be subsumed under what we might term "the interaction of any two beings.)

Three elements are involved:

1. The provision for a *space* in which one can dedicate one's whole heart and mind
2. in order to welcome the others into the exquisite flow of *time*.
3. Then a totally relaxing pause is provided for mannerly actions and conversation. The spirit of Tea sees this kind of encounter as though it discloses a whole lifetime and hence is *one life in one encounter*.

---

10. Nishitani Keiji, or in Western style, Keiji Nishitani, was of the famous Kyoto school of philosophy founded by *Nishida* Kitaro.
11. Although *sadō* is usually translated "tea ceremony," Hattori strenuously objects to the narrowness of this interpretation. What Rikyu achieved was a re-conception of the ceremony so that the way of tea became an esthetic and religious discipline rather than a showing off of oneself or one's precious wares and art acquisitions.
12. Here I see what appears to be a blending of Zen and Gabriel Marcel's influence on Hattori's thinking. However, it is to be noted that, instead, this vision may be best viewed as an instance of what Hajime Nakamura has referred to as a "parallel development," since Japanese Zen masters and practitioners influenced Hattori *before* he studied in Paris.

Afterwards, I received an answer to my question about the egocentricity of Zen. It came in the Parisian garden, Jardin Khan, while I was walking with Sen Sōshitsu, the grandmaster of Urasenske. He is a member the main family of Sen and a direct descendent of Sen Rikyū, the very first grand master. Sen Sōshitsu's direct answer:

Tea is Zen practiced by two.

There is a Zen-in-action that is the opposite of the Zen of quietness and no activity. At that moment the meaning became clear for me. The calm and peace of soul that I was seeking and that accompanies true joy is not found in solitude. Instead, what I discovered was that its precise *place* is located in the personal encounter of a lifetime in which we learn to breathe in harmony with each other and with nature.

Bridge 17

Perhaps Zen meditation helps a rigid or legalistic Japanese to "do good" naturally and spontaneously . . . . Ruth Benedict sheds light on this: "According to their philosophy man in his inmost soul is good. If his impulse can be directly embodied in his deed, he acts virtuously and easily." Therefore through training he is able "to eliminate the self-censorship of shame (*haji*)."[13] Thus, the seeming indifference of Zen to "moral principles" makes sense in the context of a too shame-regimented society.

For further reflection I give Sen Sōshitsu's motto: "Peace [from all conflict comes] through sharing a bowl of Tea." Is this too ambitious an expectation? Here's his defense:

> It is my sincere belief that in the egalitarian sharing of a bowl of tea with one's guest, a sense of peacefulness is created which can have an effect on the world. If you and your guest share that feeling of peacefulness with two others, then it will have spread to four people. If each of those four people shares it with others, and so on, the number will expand exponentially, like the ripples on the surface of a lake, creating an out-flowing of peace. . . .The essence of the phrase "Peacefulness through a Bowl of Tea" is the spirit of sharing, and it is with this motto that I have made tea for people around the world.[14]

This 15th Sen Master comments that Rikyu created in the midst of a dissolving social system "a new form of social interaction where people from all ranks of society, from lords down to farmers, could come together in a haven of peace. This was something that was very daring and revolutionary at that time."

---

13. Ruth Benedict, *The Chrysanthemum and the Sword* (Meridian Books, 1967), p. 251.
14. Consult http://nobleharbor.com/tea/chado/teachadointerview.html

18

The Encounter of a Lifetime[1]
What Rikyū Found[2]

> Sadō, the Tea Ceremony, is something born from an encounter between the samurai code (*bushidō*) and the Catholic Mass. – Sen Sōshitsu[3]

When I first heard the news of the sudden death of Madame Sen, spouse of the grand Tea Master Sen, my thoughts flew to the Khan Garden in Boulogne, a suburb in the southwestern part of Paris. The time was sometime in the mid-60s. It was early summer in the Japanese-style garden filled with the fragrance of lush greenness. The occasion was the donation of a teahouse by the Urasenke School of the Tea ceremony.[4] The house was named the Green Maple Pavilion. Many celebrities from various fields crowded one after another into the opening event. At an exhibition of correct tea ceremony procedure held in the tea house, Master Sen Soshitsu and his disciples, as well as the young ladies who assisted, were

---

1. Hattori has explained to me the Japanese maxim that guides each tea ceremony, "Act as if this were the sole *encounter* in your life." – Hattori
2. Sen Rikyū (Sen = the family name) is the 16th century founder of Sadō of which the visible part is the Tea Ceremony. What he founded, however, is an institution and ceremony based on what he *found*, a new way of looking at human encounter.
3. In Western style, Sōshitsu Sen. At the time of writing he was still the current and 15th Grand Master of the tradition founded by Sen Rikyū.
4. Urasenke is one of the two largest tea schools, Urasenke and Omotesenke. Also, we need to learn to think of the "tea ceremony" as the Way of Tea, because the thoughts,

overwhelmed by the numbers that showed up in the large Japanese garden.

Though it was a little outside my expected role as a member of the Japanese Embassy, I rushed into the preparation room in the tea pavilion and worked feverishly to help prepare tea for the large company of guests. The fact that I was formerly a member a Kyoto circle known as the Mind of Tea prepared me for the role of tea-brewer.

When I caught my breath enough to look up, I beheld a beautiful lady working to my left preparing tea. The person who was so skillfully and gracefully using the tea whisk was none other than the aforementioned Madame Tomiko Sen. Her fine-patterned kimono had such surpassing elegance she seemed to have just stepped out of a painting by the renowned poet and painter Takeshita Yumeji (1884-1934). Believe it or not, the presence of the wife of an eminent Japanese family in the area at the rear of a tea pavilion was an event possible in Paris but unthinkable in Kyoto.

Paris suited Madame Sen splendidly. Moreover, this was as it should be, for according to what she revealed to me, this talented and well-educated woman, in a time before she entered the Sen household through marriage, had seriously considered pursuing the study of literature in Paris. Her aspiration to be in Paris was manifest when she spoke to my wife in beautifully accented French.

I think that Madame Tomiko, always kimono-clad and welcomed with warmth and deference everywhere on earth, was, along with her husband, one of Japan's best citizen ambassadors. Comporting themselves with pure Japanese etiquette, their gracious decorum evidenced itself in whatever country they visited. For example, they attracted the attention of the whole staff of their hotel in a natural manner. If questioned about her whereabouts, any employee could give the correct answer.

We now shift to the year 1976 when UNESCO held its first Japanese Cultural Festival. Without any hesitation I invited the Urasenke School to grace that event. In the very center of the Japanese garden created by Isamu Noguchi, chairs had been set up for non-Japanese guests at the tea ceremony. This reserved section was surrounded by red and white curtains to create privacy in which these guests might participate in the ceremony.

On the opening day of this festival, a great many ambassadors and other dignitaries were seated in rows, and Master Sen Sōshitsu set forth the Way of Tea as the fruit of an intellectual and spiritual encounter between Japanese and Western cultures. He described how a "linkage of the samurai code (*bushidō*) and the Catholic Mass" came about. The Way of the Sword in kendo and the Way of the Bow in *kyūdō* are mirrored in the proper handling of the ladle in the

---

feelings and disciplines involved are broader than the merely social or ceremonious enjoyment of tea. Hattori concurs with this summary, commenting, "Exactly! *Dō* 道 implies the way of self-perfection."

tea ceremony. Similarly, in the elegant purification of the tea cup and the utensil containing the tea powder, there is reflected the reverent manner of the priest as he handles the sacred chalice in the Mass.

The realization that Tea creates an encounter between Japanese culture and Christianity surprised me. Nevertheless, Master Sen's comments resolve many riddles, for example, why the tea ceremony was especially popular in seminaries opened by missionaries in the 16th century or why some tea cups surviving from that era are stamped with the cross; or why the tea garden at the Imperial villa – "Detached Palace" – of Katsura in Kyoto contains Christian-style lanterns.

In the year 1549, the Jesuit Francis Xavier landed on the tip of the island of Kyushu, and with the goodwill of the feudal lord of Satsuma, set about his missionary work, which showed immediate success. Of course it was a misfortune that when he visited Kyoto he was not able to see the Emperor, but he had many contacts with local lords of the western regions who were thinking about trade with foreigners. These lords of Kyushu and Chōshū[5] accepted Xavier and Christianity to facilitate trade. Beyond all that, I believe the important factor was that Xavier was a person of superb character and power. In only two years he somehow surmounted the Japanese-language barrier. His Society of Jesus during this period is said to have produced 150,000 converts.

There was an unfortunate ban on Christianity in 1587 instigated by Toyotomi Hidyoshi, the shogun who succeeded Oda Nobunaga[6], but his own master Nobunaga during his lifetime welcomed foreign missionaries and actively sought to absorb certain features of their transoceanic culture. It is reasonable to think that Rikyu, Nobunaga's Tea Master before becoming Hideyoshi's, would have witnessed a Catholic Mass.

It can be said with utmost certainty that Saichō (767-822)[7] in the early part of the 9th century, as a member of a Japanese study mission to China, brought tea back to Japan. At first tea was for medicinal use and was offered before a Buddha sanctuary.[8] However, after the Kamakura Period (12th-14th century), when the cultivation of tea had become a widespread practice, it spread among ordinary

---

5. Chōshū is the modern Yamaguchi Prefecture at the extreme western end of the main island of Honshu.
6. Oda Nobunaga (1534-1582) was the first military Lord who almost unified Japan. Assassinated in 1582, he was succeeded in power by Hideyoshi. It is known that Nobunaga treated Christian missionaries favorably because he was curious to learn from them about was happening in the world outside Japan.
7. Saichō the founder of the Tendai school of Buddhism opened his temple on the top of Mount Hiei-san near Kyoto.
8. The classic explainer/defender of Tea to the West is Kakuzo Okakura (1863-1913). His still popular *Book of Tea* is acute in ridiculing Western criticisms and misunderstandings of Tea. A famous aphorism of his goes something like this: *How can those whose great things are small criticize those who have found small things great?*

people as a daily drink. In those days *chakai* (tea parties) were being held quite frequently in Sakai, a port of Osaka receiving foreign ships. There was a social sphere in which it was fashionable to admire – and brag about – the *karamono* (precious foreign wares) that rich merchants had acquired.

But Master Sen Rikyu, who hailed from the same circles, unexpectedly brought a mental/spiritual dimension to the heretofore largely sociable teatimes.[9] He transformed a fashionable social occasion into an opportunity for communion of spirits.

"A house, just to provide shelter from the rain; meals, in order not to starve. That's enough. This teaching is the teaching of Buddha and is identical with the real meaning of the way of tea" (*cha-no-yu*).

The *wabicha*[10] of Master Sen was a spiritual revolution. We may consider it to have involved a significant cultural encounter. His world approaches Zen in an ever closer way. What's more, such a world has much in common with the discipline of bushido.

In that connection, the person who walks quietly along the clean-swept lane of a tea garden approaches Tea in the right way because he or she is staying close to the essence of Bushido (the Samurai code) and Zen. After cleansing body and soul at a stone basin, the tea participant stoops to enter the tearoom through its tiny door, thus humbling body and soul. At that time, the man or woman dispenses with all baggage of social status or class consciousness and becomes just one human being. Even the samurai leaves his sword outside. In the tearoom the participant finds a space cut off from the ordinary routine of daily life. And there the host of the ceremony has a time of "communion" with the guest, as if the moment has become the sole encounter of a lifetime.

The Mass or Lord's Supper is a reproduction of Jesus' last meal with his disciples. By means of the wine and the bread a person is united with Jesus. I think of the Way of Tea as an *encounter of a lifetime* that is also a form of spiritual communion. These recollections and reflections – along with the image of her beautiful image – quietly permeated my heart and mind when I heard of the too early death of Madame Tomiko Sen.

Bridge 18

I've talked with several persons about this chapter who are closer than I to Roman Catholic ritual and practice. I have asked one of these, my American

---

9. It is perhaps well to note that Master Sen Rikyu (not to be confused with Hattori's contemporary, Sen Sōshitsu) had seven principal disciples, three of whom were Christian.
10. Etymologically, *wabi-cha* means abstemious tea.

Catholic friend, Jerry Aistrup to comment here:

> Having participated in a traditional Japanese tea ceremony in 1991 I can say that I had no thought at that time that this experience resembled receiving communion during a Catholic Mass. But this observation must be tempered by the fact that what I was participating in was not well explained.[11] I also lean toward the belief in the universality of all spiritual expression so this would not make it hard to accept the author's linking of the two experiences.[12]

Most tourists only know the social aspect of tea, but the metaphysical and esthetic depths explored by the Mind of Tea Circle in its relationship to communion in the Mass has been noted by many foreign scholars, but Hattori adds, "The event in Paris was the first time the fact was noted by the Grand Master himself."

Hattori once explained to me how his mother had him take lessons in the Way of Tea when he was but a Middle School boy. "Even now I am grateful to my mother for that exposure, for it permitted me to join the Shincha-kai of Kyoto." He went on to explain how that experience equipped him to help Master and Madame Sen later in Paris.

"The house of Mr. and Mrs. Sen – *Konnichi-An*, Pavilion of Today – provided a truly wonderful space for my wife and myself. Madame Sen received just the two of us in a private tea ceremony. It is unthinkable even now that she would have so honored us ordinary people.... Moreover, I must say out of both pleasure and duty that my wife, who is French, has on such occasions found these encounters be without parallel elsewhere."

Even as a student visiting various Japanese temples in Kyoto Hattori noticed a linkage between Japanese Tea and Christianity. Then in Paris as a graduate student he noticed the same connection in attending various masses and also several Protestant communion services

Hattori adds, "The reproduction of the Last Supper in such churches is completely identical with the proper way of drinking dark, strong Tea." The deep meaning of the shared chalice in modern Catholicism, he points out, is comparable to samurai sharing tea before battle. And, finally: "It is not by chance that Master Sen Sōshitsu, who has informed the world about these matters, received the designation of Honorary Consul-General of Portugal."

---

11. Hattori is not surprised. In response he writes, "The average foreign visitor has no occasion to participate in a meeting like our Mind of Tea circle." He further explains that the tea host creates a perfect moment and space like the Mass, not an intimate social occasion.
12. Mr. Aistrup is a retired history teacher, a community leader, and president of the Cowley County Historical Society, hence director of its museum located in Winfield, Kansas, USA.

19

Rationale for the Elimination of Collectivism[1]
Concerning the Culture of Shame

> The universal character of humanity is first found at points where humans live their own existence deeply. The individual buried in a group is a mere ghost image and hence will never encounter universal humankind.

1995 was the International Year of Tolerance. However, in Japan almost nothing happened. Is that because most Japanese thought that only other countries are beset by conflagrations of intolerance, fires that ignite blood-shedding disputes over ethnic or religious differences? On the religious front where the relationship of the divine and human is involved, Japan is certainly tolerant. However, how does Japan measure up in terms of the relationship of one human to another in the moral dimension?

I would like somehow to blend into this question the issue of the tendency toward "collectivism" prevalent in this country. The fundamental fact is that collectivism is a morality without tolerance.

In the postwar period there was a famous book by Ruth Benedict, *The Chrysanthemum and the Sword* (1948). The gist of her book is that in the West there is a "culture of guilt" while in Japan there is a "culture of shame." It is possible to refute details in her analysis, but right now it will be worthwhile to try to penetrate the core of her distinction between the two cultures. The Christian

---

1. The Japanese word in the title is a compound composed literally of "group" + "ism."

idea of "original sin" has never become more than mere knowledge for the Japanese. Even *the consciousness of sins or crimes committed against God* had not yet come into existence among the Japanese. In contrast to sin in this absolute sense, we Japanese are stubbornly relativistic, that is, "Crimes committed by humans are something relative." (The word "crimes" here is closely associated with subjective feelings of guilt or shame in relation to one's group.) Whatever is treated in Western Europe as "evil" becomes "dirty" in Japan. It is not something that must be expiated but cleansed.

Father Bona, a priest who had studied Zen and Shinto in Japan, returned to France as a Japanophile. He explained, "In Japan God is not *bon Dieu* (goodness) but *beau Dieu* (beauty)." This means that the value at the bottom of Japanese consciousness finds the important opposition to be *beauty vs. ugliness*, not goodness vs. evil.

The viewpoint of Ruth Benedict is deeply involved with the issues of Chapter 3 above, as anyone glancing at its title, "To Be or to Appear," will see. While *the very being of a person* is the problem at issue in a "culture of guilt" as it relates to one's own individual and subjective[2] actions, the problem in a culture of shame is how *one appears to others*.

In Japan there are all kinds of communities in which the group exerts a powerful influence on individuals through the connections found in all groupings: villages and feudal domains in former times; and today companies, schools, government offices and public corporations. Visiting one of these groups, we can a see at a glance a kind of calm and harmonious "equality." Such equality is not true equality but rather uniformity. A slightly different or strange[3] person will soon be removed from the group. "The nail that sticks up will be hammered down" and "A skilful hawk hides its claws" are sayings that are considered eternal verities.

A school or office uniform suits this kind of society. Recently, youth have been parading strange dress in neighborhoods once soberly or even stuffily residential. It is ironically sad the extent to which the young people wish to conform to the collective "appeal of individual identity." It is best to see their weird appearance as a rather tiny show of defiance toward the uniform.

The collectivism reflected in wearing a uniform is superficially sweet and dependable, but because of its uniformization[4] it is a smoke screen for the bullying that always attacks any variation from group norms. And, worse still, it conceals

---

2. "Subjective" in the sense that Western guilt encourages honest doubt about one's own actions and their possibly hurtful or helpful consequences; it relates much less to group approval.
3. The idiom here literally refers to someone who has changed hair color.
4. The *Oxford English Dictionary* recognizes this unusual word, which Hattori prefers for the translation of *shūdantai*. It suggests an ongoing process and not simply a kind of static belief or onetime practice such as "collectivism" may do.

the possibility that for one group another will be "outside," "foreign," or "the enemy."

Therefore, in Japan there is an expression that is never translated into a foreign language: "Truly there is no excuse for you to disturb society." At the time of frequent disasters in the political or financial world, such words are often heard. The equivocal expression, "I regret it" is also used. What is behind such words is the feeling that *I'm not bad because I've done a bad thing; I'm bad because it's being disclosed to society.* The bad that stays within one's group is not so bad.[5] The bad becomes really bad only when it is revealed by the media. This is the essence of the "culture of shame." In short what doesn't "appear" or become public doesn't exist.

Anyone wanting to stay in good standing must comply with the group's instinct of self-defense. To comply means to avoid revealing group faults to the outside world, never betraying the group in any way. All matters must be arranged quietly, and so in this situation there is the opportunity for a special kind of gangster called *sōkaiya* to appear. (Such a person will manage, even manipulate, a general meeting of stockholders.) By the way, there is no English translation for this peculiar Japanese word *sōkaiya*. American newspapers simply print it as SOKAIYA in association with YAKUZA (hooligan or hoodlum).[6]

If other countries do not trust Japanese companies, it is not so much because the companies need ten persons instead of one to arrive at a decision, but rather that almost all employees sent to foreign countries are unable to get acclimated to the people and culture of the host country. Hence employees are constantly looking toward Tokyo, thus showing their incurable "groupism." The fact must be noted that groupism cannot be a principle of fraternity (the feeling of connection with all other human beings). Collectivism, being too narrow to house any principle of benevolence or humanity, is essentially a culture of intolerance based on the logic of exclusiveness toward the outsider. Exactly for that reason, every form of groupism or collectivism in world history has been doomed to the lethal fate of any isolationism that hates everything and everybody different from itself. We Japanese ought to face squarely the fate of Japanese militarism of the past, as well as Nazism, fascism, and Stalinism – or the frantically destructive Red Guard movement in China.

---

5. A crass American saying goes, "I don't regret what I did, but I do regret being caught at it."
6. These two words are troublesome because, though related, they are by no means synonymous. For a high-quality glimpse into American scholarship on this subject see the website of the Japan Society of New York, especially the stunning 2002 lecture by Kenneth Szymkowiak, professor of Criminal Justice in Chaminade University in Honolulu. Japansociety.org/sokaiya, accessed 8-4-2008. We'll say more in our Bridge below.

The universality of humanity is only discovered at the very moment when a human being deeply lives his or her human existence. The individual who is buried in a group is an illusion, an image or ineffectual ghost and as such never really touches or enjoys universal humanity. A person limited to being just an "appearance" or expression of something else (in this case, the group) has only a "virtual" existence.

Perhaps sometime there will be a period in which *beauty* becomes the standard of value instead of *goodness*. However, it is not at all clear, to say the least, how much the suicide of Yukio Mishima, ritualized as his unique aesthetics, conveys the same universal value as Dostoevsky's *Crime and Punishment*.

Bridge 19

For anyone who perhaps never heard of Mishima's efforts to resurrect Japanese tradition through writing, martial arts and activities – and ultimately through suicide – some explanation is in order here. When Buddhist disciplines designed to free devotees from all fear of suffering and death merge with the Japanese warrior's sense of loyalty to his lord or emperor, even to the point of ritual suicide because of insult to the lord or failure to defend him – you have the essence of the kind of thinking that produced Mishima's highly visible and controversial suicide, performed as carefully as possible in the prescribed manner. Suicide in Japanese tradition is diametrically opposed to most Western doctrines on the subject. Hattori's point above is that, in broadly human terms, a traditionally "aesthetic suicide" is an instance of "Beauty" demoting "the Good."

We two authors believe that this demotion should now be renounced, not just from a Western humanist or Christian point of view, but from a global transversal of values.

To sum up the matter, Mishima was one of the greatest of the authors of postwar Japan. His work and life, taken together, were a single esthetic creation. In the light of this whole chapter it is appropriate to wonder whether a ritually correct or "esthetically" executed suicide is necessarily a "good" suicide, or, for that matter, a good act.

Just to complicate things in order to disclose how really complex comparative studies get, I'll now quote what Hattori wrote me about Mishima as I tried to make closure for us:

> Mishima is the last samurai in Japanese literature. He committed Seppuku to protest against the corruption of the Japanese spirit. He has nothing in common with Yakuza, the Japanese gangster. Mishima was noble.

Perhaps so, but was he or was he not too "esthetic" in his nobility? Soren Kierkegaard, for one, would say so. In his Western, Christian mode, I think Hattori would agree but . . . .

* * *

What about the *Sōkaiya*? And the related *Yakuza*?
Due to the openness of shareholders' meetings, this special kind of gangster can blackmail a board into doing unwise, unlawful or unethical things. The *sōkaiya* (singular or plural) can and do threaten to disrupt the public meetings thus discrediting the company. To avoid this, Hattori observes, "Companies even pay them." The gangs in Japan are different from Mafia-like mobs in the West; but in one respect they are the same. For a mob member to go out on his own involves a contradiction in terms. Such an individual in the West, instead of remaining a gangster, may quickly become dead. In Japan he may have a finger cut off.

Hattori has pertinent comments on some related issues. "The wives of yakuza society are themselves yakuza. Their various units constitute a special society with its own rules." Their loyalty to their group is similar to samurai loyalty to their class, though in other respects they and samurai are totally different. "They are a sort of gangster with their territories but, generally, they do not harm normal people."

The gang's fear of publicity, and also the board members', is generally greater than any moral constraint against doing wrong. Often the wrongdoing comes out anyway sooner or later, and the disgrace for the "respectable" is even greater. While I was a visiting professor in Japan in 1997-98, there was a series of exposures. Night after night on the evening news somber government officials were seen carrying out all records from headquarters. One evening's TV footage on the scandals could have been repeated for all the rest of them, but the cumulative effect of this publicity for the public must have been daunting. It may even have produced a widespread collective sense of exposure and shame. One fact lessening the impact on the respectable was that the *sokaiya* were not members of the board and could thus be used as scapegoats for some of the things that were brought to light.

Hattori summarizes, "The point of this chapter is that collectivism is the logic of exclusion. . . ." Americans might note that in our marketplace the large American companies also act by this logic. Consequently, other companies and even ordinary citizens become their enemy, if we judge by their actions.

20

Families with No Alpha Figure
Dynamics of a Boy's Crime

The boy who was killed with a metal bat by his father was not seeking a parent who would surrender to his every demand. He must have been looking for a real parent who could *resolutely fill the role of an alpha* (a family leader).

This affair was unusual because the father who killed his son was a normal man, a tender individual. He decided to kill his son after years and years of domestic violence. During this period the son was ordering the family about and even beating his parents . . . . Let us try to explain the psychology of such a boy. Violence, we feel, must be approached gently to be understood.[1]

Now when I close my eyes what comes to the surface like a faint vision is a beautiful piece of framed calligraphy with the words:

> I trace a vine
> with lily fingers
> I trace back a vine

Tracing Back . . .

In a personal note to me our author suggests that the "tracing back" of this poem may refer to a painful memory, and, at the same time, to a possible source of help. – WG

---

1. Lacking in the original, this paragraph is added as the necessary frame for our revamped chapter.

The vision I had as a young man came to me while I was secluded in my room in the boarding house. Who left that frame in my room? As I reflect on this, the figure floating up to my memory is a certain fairy lady. Was it she who left the calligraphy? In contrast to that memory, which was sadly fading like the light at dusk, the words in that art work are agitating my mind as if they represent some kind of appeal. Their very vividness encourages me to suppose that they depict some kind of outcry. The white finger of the poem's author reminds me of a girl tracing or retracing something – but what?

Recently there have been many sayings like the tracing or retracing finger: "He must have been looking for help, don't you think?" This question was part of the testimony of the classmate of a boy who tried to rob and kill a police officer.

And consider the word of the father referred to in our leading quotation. He recalls the son's face during an outbreak of his violence.

"I could see from my son's face as he was beating me that he was crying." Such words break my heart as we continue to face a nationwide increase of juvenile delinquency in Japan.

Why would a young boy be *kireru*,[2] that is, so *broken off* from society that he turns violent? "The schools are bad." "Society is bad." Various criticisms such as these are put forward, but for me an important point is missing in all of them – or perhaps it has merely been made light of. As far as our lives are concerned, we human beings, particularly in adolescence, are essentially unstable creatures. This period is an uneasy time in which one is seeking an "authoritative grounding," a place of security and peace of mind. And such a place is none other than the home.

The home where a person is formed, even when no longer lived in, exists in one's heart. Peace there is indispensable. However, it is not enough for that peace to merely be a peace in which nothing happens. *Peace of mind* (a feeling of security) must more and more prevail. It is only with peace of mind that peace becomes happiness.

Because of the historic importance of Euro-American individualism and Japanese familism, it is no wonder that too many people have the vague sense that *homes* (strong families) abound in Japan. However, in reality they do not. Presently there is no country in the world in which the home is in a greater state of collapse than in Japan. There is little doubt that in Asia and Africa, and even in America and Europe, there is more of a close home tie than in Japan. In these areas outside Japan it is an exception for husband-fathers to return home in the

---

2. The word 切れる *kireru* has many such meanings. Author Hattori adds that the word キレル – same pronunciation but sometimes written in this phonetic script rather than as an ideogram – is essentially a new word with specific reference to a younger person. In old-fashioned English we used to say of such individuals that they "had a nervous breakdown" or "went berserk."

dead of night, as is usual in Japan. In those areas, but not in Japan, most families are together on weekends.[3]

In Japan, in one sense, a man is doubly married – to his wife and to his company. Therefore, there are fatherless homes, although the father should occupy the center of the home. I like to describe this phenomenon, as the "home of alpha's absence."

"Alpha" refers to the fact that a dog or wolf pack naturally selects a leader. There is a time of struggle for this alpha position, but it reflects the wisdom of nature for the survival of the pack. I have learned a fact that occurs in Japan and has never, or less frequently, been heard of in Europe or America. It's the fact that dogs will bite family members. Specialists in canine psychology explain why dogs act this way.

First is the fact that such a dog sees the people in a human family as the dog's own pack. However, when he perceives no alpha in this group, the dog thinks the pack is in danger unless he accepts the role himself. Then he bites. In the opposite situation where there is an alpha – male or female – the dogs are obedient and do not bite. A dog that is strictly disciplined may seem pathetic to an outsider. In reality that dog is happy, for he has peace of mind and feels secure in this well-ordered group.

We must reflect on the fact that all animals protect the security and safety of the family group; as human beings we must aspire to that same intention and mode of living. If we are to do this, we will be able to see the core of the problem, because we will be taking into account the whole picture of juvenile delinquency in its earliest and primal setting.

As we mentioned at the beginning of this chapter, the troubled boy must have been looking for someone to be his alpha parent – some person or persons who would act firmly, thus manifesting an intense and positive feeling for human existence.

Just being present is totally different from a parental flaunting of authority that degenerates into yelling or hitting. The *presence* will survive even a parent's death. At the Olympic Games held in Nagano in 1998 the parents still existed in the hearts of the two young athletes who got gold medals. (Both athletes felt their deceased fathers watching them.) Shimizu, a male skater, won the gold in the 500 meter, and the young woman Satoya won it in mogul skiing.

The youth who lacks this sense of peace and security at home will join a gang at school to obtain it either from the leader or from the pack itself. Or, as a loner, he'll himself attempt to substitute for the alpha and then launch himself

---

3. One American phenomenon mirrors the "absence of an alpha figure." It is the so-called blended family. The child whose last name is a puzzle because of the divorces and remarriages of his biological or adoptive parents may not know how to express his frustrations. He may not even know how to ask the forcefully plaintive question, "Who the hell am I?"

into a well-concealed quest for revenge and self-destruction. At that point a transmutation of the gold of a boy's potential will have been transmuted into a bully's leaden cruelty, a ticking bomb for himself and society.

Bridge 20

According to Hattori's "Note,"

> Aristotle in his De Anima theorizes that the "soul" of animals is higher than that of plants. Before Aristotle, the soul in any one thing was equal to the soul in anything else (similar to the persisting notion of mana in the Polynesian religions – and Shinto). When I think about this, I feel that since everything in the prior stages of evolution is connected with homo sapiens, why shouldn't the mode of living of the other animals be considered whenever we look at social problems?

Eiji summarizes his conviction in these words: "The soul or vital principle of the animal contains that of the plant, and the soul of Homo Sapiens contains that of the animal and the plant. Human beings can benefit by looking downward as well as upward!"

Hattori goes on to explain how there is no "big tree" in the schools for a child to lean on. Teachers do not have time to fulfill much of the steady-tree responsibility. They are more like friends or servants to the children, and when they try to take the place of a family authority figure, they step out of their role and veer away from a true educational path.

* * *

WG: Davion, when I recently met your mother, it occurred to me that she is an admirable alpha figure. Since your dad sort of faded from the picture while you were an adolescent, do you feel she perhaps was all the alpha-figure you needed?

D: I definitely have to give my mother a lot of credit for filling that role in my family, but even though she did an excellent job, she was still a female, and nobody can truly show a boy how to be manly except a man, so I was always seeking shelter under the wings of an older male alpha figure. Unfortunately some of my role models have been bad . . . .

WG: I respect your testimony here. Personally I would prefer not to limit the alpha idea too literally to gender. Can you help us, Eiji?

H: In any country, it is easy and usually correct to link juvenile delinquency to the absence of a *real family*. A family united by love that has a trunk/an alpha/ a moral center is what I consider a real family.

WG: While attending activities surrounding our younger grandson's graduation from Boulder High School, I encountered in a Boulder newspaper (*Daily Camera*, May 26, 2008, 4B) an eloquent example of *a family united by love*, a family with *a strong moral center*.

In Lafayette, Colorado, when Siena Faughnan, 14, might have been looking forward to a leisurely summer vacation sleeping in late, spending time at the pool, and the like, she opted instead to devote much of June 2008 "helping establish computer access for the 450 students at the K-9 Ejisu Model School" in hot and humid Ejisu, Ghana. In addition, she chose to teach students how to use certain software programs; she also arranged to install a solar power system to supplement the erratic supply of electric power in Ghana.

A year earlier, at age 13, she had "helped set up 100 computers . . . shipped to Ejisu by World Computers Exchange." The *Camera* article described in some detail the support of Siena by various family members, including Siena's mother, Cathy.

Cathy comments that such experiences are giving her daughter "a perspective of what we have in this country. It's interesting that she sees how happy they are over there and that wealth doesn't equate to happiness." Faughnan lost her husband Chris on 9/11/2001. She explains that the tragedy helped push her and her three children toward "acts of international healing."

21

Educating People to Think for Themselves
Good Uses for "Useless" Leisure

The word "school" derives from the Greek scholé (σχολή, spare time, leisure). People moved to think for themselves during their times of leisure are like minds reborn; such individuals are the ones who have created culture.

What must Japanese young people be thinking when they have to begin their school year in April during cherry blossom time?! Isn't that a time to relax in a festive way with friends and family while soaking up the evanescent beauty?

Early in 1997 President Clinton in his State of the Union address to Congress spoke out for the necessity of a bipartisan effort to improve education.[1] In part, Clinton said, "Let's work together to meet these . . . goals: Every 8-year-old must be able to read; every 12-year-old must be able to log on to the Internet; every 18-year-old must be able to go to college; and every adult American must be able to keep on learning for a lifetime."

Surely it is a serious social problem in the great nation of America that there has been a sudden increase of young people who on finishing school have simply forgotten how to write (if they ever learned) to the extent that 20% are "functionally illiterate."[2] (Tersely put, functional illiteracy refers to adults who

---

1. From Part 2 of the full transcript of the speech. It may be accessed at www.cnn.com/2005/ALLPOLITICS/01/31/sotu.clinton1997/index.html.
2. There are at least three degrees of illiteracy. *Functional illiteracy* is the lack of basic skills in reading, writing, and mathematics. *Cultural illiteracy* is absence of the skills

cannot read and write well enough to function in a modern society.)

In contrast, it is said that in Japan the rate of illiteracy doesn't even reach 1%. Should we simply assume that all the credit for this goes to Japan's educational system so that it obviously needs no reform? This question is crucial to where we are headed in this chapter, but before answering it, we wish to explain and support the contrast just drawn.

President Clinton's numbers need to be updated because of the passage of time, and ours, too, need refinement and substantiation. We must not take the time here to defend or update every number mentioned, but we can cite a summary of now-current percentages and their sources:

> In the United States, according to *Business* magazine, an estimated 15 million functionally illiterate adults held jobs at the beginning of the 21st century. The American Council of Life Insurers reported that 75% of the Fortune 500 companies provide some level of remedial training for their workers. All over [the] U.S.A. 40-45 million (21% of adults) are functionally illiterate.[3]

The Japanese educational system, which is admired for its period of growth and development, helped achieve a place for Japan among the great economic powers of the world. That is because it produces uniform individuals, who all work and act predictably according to regulations, like ants. This kind of life is perceived by the rest of the world as an existence that is both wonderful and weird. Herein lies an underlying cause of the phenomenon known as "Japan bashing." Therefore, when the bubble burst and the eye of the economic typhoon passed over all of Southeast Asia, then "Japan bashing" came to the fore due to Japan's acting in indifferent and uncaring ways.

We don't need to inform readers of the EU, an organic union of European states. What is on the rise, in a big way, is a consciousness of regional solidarity within and across national boundaries. Furthermore, it is widely perceived in the early 21st century that if the human species is to continue to live on this precious earth, all nations and all races must awake to the importance of a symbiosis that means *both letting all the others live and even helping them live*. We all are continuing to enter the so-called period of globalization.

However, I often happen upon newspaper articles claiming that the Japanese lack any feeling of joint responsibility, have no sense of solidarity with others, and hence are capable of no true friendship. The tone of such arguments abundantly illustrates why the general public finds politics *unsavory*, but I think the real problem is with the consciousness of Japanese *individuals*. The "parent" that generates this negative feeling about social or global responsibility is education.

---

and knowledge necessary to "thrive in the modern world." *Moral illiteracy* and *spiritual illiteracy* are terms of deficiency for their respective spheres. Accessed on 4-22-05 at www.reformed.org/web files/antithesis/v1n5ant_v1n5_illiteracy.html.

3. http://en.wikipedia.org/wiki/Functional_illiteracy.

And, as one might suspect, the central actor in shaping thinking so irresponsibly is the school system. Therefore, in Japan in order to avoid walking the path of isolationism, we must question and even reprove the essence of Japanese public school education as presently constituted. I ask, "Really now, where is the best place to form a good and skilled citizen?"

If a person is roaming the world, he or she is bound to become globally aware, but even though Africa and Asia contain countries that are economically poor, the children's eyes sparkle brightly. Japanese children are blessed in all material things, but their eyes lack sparkle. Educators in particular ought to pay attention to this absence of sparkle. A system of education and testing that is totally devoid of originality produces gray-suited commuters on the train or tram who are hard to distinguish one from another. During their lifetime such individuals for the $10,000^{th}$ time will hear a voice requesting, "Because of the danger, please step behind the white line." By this kind of conditioning, they are best suited to obey quietly and obediently what they are told to do. Unless this country also is trying intentionally to form citizens who are "easy to rule,"[4] it must consider this problem very seriously.

A French visitor to Japan, after returning home from Kobe, wrote back, "There were no Japanese faces there. There were the faces of humanity." A *human face* is one that feels for itself, thinks for itself, and decides for itself. The university was where I discovered that. The reason is, now that the hurdle of "examination hell" had been passed, the university was the place where I may have had the last chance to *shape my humanity*.

I often speak in this way to university students at the beginning of a new term:

"As for the university, it's the place that forms you as a human being capable of thinking for yourself as an individual. Up to this time you've heard a teacher saying, 'Now boys and girls, attention!' He or she hoped you would be receptive to studying and *learning*. However, now, from this point on, you will be expected to become more active in *investigating* and *researching*. Research is an intellectual activity involving thinking and reflecting on your own. I cannot teach you philosophy. What I am supposed to teach you is how to *philosophize* for yourself. You have four years of college and after that, for an average of 60 years, there will be no teacher. For the benefit of the life ahead of you, I would like to help awaken your powers to think for yourself."

"However," I continue, "if this is to happen, it is important for you to have time for *asobi* (play, leisure, relaxation). As a matter of fact, philosophy was born in playful chatter. The ones conversing in the city square were slaveholding free citizens. For them this was *free time*. In other words, such time afforded them scope for relaxation and playfulness. The difference between a citizen and a slave

---

4. This expressive phrase is matched by the American saying, "He's just a yes-man."

did not primarily lie in one's "job description" but rather in "having time of one's own."

The etymology of "school" is *scholé* (Greek, specifically referring to leisure for learning). Compare the German *Schule*, French *école*, and Latin *schola*. People who think for themselves and experience things directly are in part "born" from leisure. Such people have created culture. Even in prewar Japan, it was like that in the senior high schools where young people argued boisterously, sang noisily, and collided with each other mentally and physically.

Some time ago there was a report from a special commission investigating education. The report stressed that the importance of the Greek *scholé* had been forgotten. To abolish culture, outlawing *playtime* alone is not enough; the elimination must be done in the name of what is called "efficiency." Then there will no longer be any opportunity for one's mind to become free. A "market principle" will have enslaved it. The university should operate as far from this market principle as possible, should it not?

What the ancient Greeks felt about the *usefulness of the useless* is once again coming into its own as something of unlimited importance.

Bridge 21

An American addicted to computers and computer games may think he is using his leisure creatively, but computer nerds seem to be compulsive about *efficiency* in gamesmanship, as much as any merchant is about profit. The pursuit of wins is a poor substitute for thinking about social or philosophical issues. It is no substitute for face-to-face conversation. "Slavishly devoted" and "socially inept" are two dictionary phrases that exactly fit nerdy people.

I believe Hattori's Note to his Japanese readers is actually a bridge to the best educational future for all of us.

In brief, he argues that Japanese university entrance exams limit themselves unnecessarily to the written word. He faults the whole educational system for too much emphasis on the answers others have come up with rather than the ability to search or research for new and better answers to our most urgent human questions.

Specifically, he extols the French thesis system as worthy of consideration for Japanese universities. It utilizes both a written thesis on a topic such as world peace and oral questions and answers about the topic. He calls this "the very best way to cultivate the capacity of the Japanese to think for oneself."

> If the present university system were to be changed, high school education would also change for the better. In France the philosophical problem posed in the examination of one's thesis for a bachelor's degree constitutes the whole of the qualifying exam, and no other standard is applied. The criticism that

the thesis defense, when subjectively evaluated by judges, will inevitably be unfair is heard in Japan, but such a criticism is never raised in France. A least four professors evaluate each thesis paper. The work of grading becomes a huge task, but it is accomplished thoroughly and in good order.

Why can what is done in France not be possible in Japan? The issue remains essentially the same in the case of an oral interrogation. It may be supposed that their system is one reason why France, with half the population of Japan, has produced three times Japan's number of Nobel Prize recipients.

22

Searching for Lost Times
The Last Words of Emperor Showa
1926-1989

> If the trade on the Silk Road lasted a thousand years, it is because each of the peoples using it realized the mutual advantage of the principle of *sharing* by the relay method in cooperation with all the other peoples involved.

Janus is the god of the year[1] according to Roman mythology. This god has one face that looks back and another that looks ahead. Janus looks back on what has transpired prior to the turning point of the year as well as forward toward the year to come. In English the first month of the calendar is called January, meaning, the "month of Janus."

As a young person, my thinking was drawn to the two faces of Janus. And recently, by dint of hard effort, I have come to the conviction that *the very act of staring hard at the past enables us to see a way to the future*.

In 1987, when it was my task to announce to the press in Paris UNESCO'S project of an Integral Study of the Silk Roads, I stated, "We are about to *sail in search of time lost*.[2] It was a time of cultural tolerance when people respected the cultures of other peoples."

---

1. Also, the god of doorways and beginnings.
2. Referring to Proust's *À la recherche du temps perdu*, known in English as *Remembrance of Things Past*.

The Silk Road that began to tie together the continent of Eurasia on an East-West axis was a main artery of cultural interchange that, before long, was building up a global civilization.³ However, two thousand years earlier, what drove people to open up a route on the high seas? We need to know also why people later opened up the land routes despite the impediment of high mountains and white-hot deserts.

From long thought and many years spent corroborating the facts, I have come up with the following:

1. The Silk Roads were not for selling. People were traveling in search of something precious, for example, fine goods, gems, silk items, even precious sutras.
2. They did not scheme to monopolize trade. They knew the value of *sharing*.⁴
3. There were no national borders, and trade was an international activity that introduced many cultures to each other by the intermingling of many peoples from the various areas of Eurasia.

What we speak of as "international" was not born in modern times. On the contrary, I quickly discovered that what is truly international has been extinguished during modern times whenever selfish nationalism, linked to the nation-state concept, has reared its ugly head.

International activity is neither a matter of imposing one's own values on others nor of forcing monopoly upon others. On the Silk Roads it was an activity that involved both learning of, and going in search of, fine things. Persian caravans crossed deserts seeking silk, Arabian ships crossed oceans on a quest for perfumes and spices, and young Japanese priests set out for Ch'ang-an (Xian, capital of Tang Dynasty) to learn the Way of Buddha. All these were risking death in their journey over deserts and seas. The persons who opened the Road were of a mind to seek *something more precious than products or goods*. I began to understand the fact that, if the Silk Road trade endured for more than a thousand years, it was because the people involved in it knew the principle of "good in a threefold direction" *sanbō yoshii* (三方よし).⁵ This required a relay system for *sharing*

---

3. For details and background information see Eiji Hattori, *Letters from the Silk Roads*, especially Chapter 2, "The Silk Roads and Peace." (University Press of America, 2000.)
4. With the advent of the internet, shareware, and other features of the information age, the importance of sharing has been given new life.
5. In a note to me, Dr. Hattori has explained this intriguing phrase to mean, "good for you, me, and them" – you my trading partner, me from afar, and the people in between who enabled us to get together.

among the seller,[6] buyer and those who enabled them to pass. This last category includes people who allowed Silk Road traffic to pass certain points, the regional lords who built caravan sarais.

In October of 1988, after all kinds of preparations were made, a first-of-its-kind Silk Road Seminar was opened. The place was the National Museum of Ethnology in Osaka directed by Tadao Umesa, who spearheaded the project. In a conference publicized far and wide by the media, all eminent figures in Japan in the field of Silk Road studies were present. The French scholar Vadime Elisseeff became leader of the delegates from the 20 participating nations of the world, along with 30 specialists – all sent by UNESCO to participate in three days of heated discussions. In the opening ceremony, I explained the gist of the plan, and soon after that we heard some formal words from Imperial Prince Mikasa. I learned afterwards that the imperial prince, having found out about this seminar via press releases, applied to participate by postcard. Hastily the astonished sponsors and promoters of the conference requested him to make a formal statement to the conference. I learned also that he had typed his pronouncement on his own word processor.

In fact, we could see the prince seated among the other delegates during the afternoon session as well during following sessions, listening eagerly to all presentations. While speaking for the opening ceremony, Prince Mikasa made an important observation. "What is most important to study is not the goods themselves but the *people* who made them, the people who carried them East and West, and the people who used them." This is certainly true. Silk Road studies are a *Study of Man* – humanity. However, what I would especially like to record here is the precious testimony set forth by the Prince before the above suggestion:

> Yesterday morning (October 22) I made a visit to my eldest brother (His majesty) who is ill. He felt unusually fine that day. When we spoke of this seminar he showed great interest displaying deep emotion about the questions concerning the land and sea routes. And, in a nostalgic tone, he asked, "Was not the terminus of the Silk Roads Rome?"

This report from a younger brother's own mouth hit me like a thunderbolt!

It came to me strongly that His Majesty, too, was thinking of *roads of dialogue*. Imagine that! "Roads to Rome. . . ."

---

6. Hattori's use of "seller" here might seem to contradict his first principle above: *The Silk Roads were not for selling*. However, by means of the full Silk Road perspective you may use "buyer" and "seller" for understanding his points as long as it is clear that each person or caravan going out is primarily a seeker of the precious in its own right rather than for monopoly or imperial expansion, or for national, military, or economic advancement of selfish interests.

My astonishment was also due to these being among the last words pronounced by Emperor Showa. It became his last official announcement through his own brother.

Three months later His Majesty the Emperor passed away, having endured and survived some of the major commotions of the 20th century. During a chilly shower that became a cloudburst, television displayed the gathering of heads of state that came from every corner of the world for the imperial funeral. When I returned to Paris, I was watching TV, while under my windows the lights of Montparnasse sparkled. I was thinking of the last pronouncement by our Emperor Hirohito, which symbolized "the dialogue of cultures." I wonder whether perhaps His Majesty also might have been *looking for lost times*.

Bridge 22

While Hattori's use of the term *sarai* in this chapter will be clear to scholars concerned with the history of the Silk Road, general readers may appreciate a short explanation here. The Oxford English Dictionary explains that a sarai (or serai) is a building to accommodate travelers, a caravanserai. Sharing was so much a part of the Silk Road culture (which was almost a civilization, certainly a civilizing agent) that a caravan could stay three days without charge, for the travelers would share what they knew and what they were carrying. The lords who built these sarai knew the value of the information brought by caravan. In *Letters from the Silk Roads*, Hattori goes further to explain (pp.17-18) that each lord knew that the "passing of the caravans was a profitable, even a divine blessing."

In recent times many successive actions have exactly negated the triform "soul" of the Silk Road. These anti-sharing actions did not seek out goods and precious things so much as try to push others to accept the values of invaders.

In this connection, it is important to understand the ambiguity of the Japanese word for "sell," because it does not exist in the single English word for selling. English requires two or more words such as "high-pressure selling" or "hard sell" to match what the Japanese implies by the word *uritsukeru*, which can denote "push," "sell," and even "force a thing upon someone."

While the English title for the UNESCO project, "Integral Study of the Silk Roads," is correct, the project itself had an even broader scope than the word "Roads" indicates. *Integral* emphasizes a concern for a whole era, area and system of exchange that was truly *one* system by land *and* sea – of goods and of the intercultural communication of philosophies and religions, tools, technologies, and general information.

Hattori's Japanese word 総合 (*sōgō*, literally "synthesis" or "coordination") makes the breadth of the endeavor in the present era even clearer. Historians, archaeologists, and students of culture have cooperated in discovering historic intercontinental or Eurasian unities. Even the news media became an *integral* part of the endeavor, to repeat the first word in the English title of the project.

Hattori believes that the contest among European powers for preeminence in the increasingly global struggle for empire prefigured the World Wars of the 20th century and, indeed, the Terrorism and the War on Terrorism in the 21st. However he ends his Note to Japanese readers on this more positive note:

> Therefore, I wonder whether that spirit of peaceful trade, which held sway for more than a thousand years, might return once more and be instructive for our human future.

Butterflies and Fireflies

Butterflies of hope open their lovely daylight wings. During the dark hours, fireflies give glints of Truth wrapped simply in *being better informed* and *slightly more understanding*.

Part III
The Tree of Life

Russell as Life's Arborist

On May 9, 2008, at College Hill Coffee shop where I imbibe regularly, I noted Bertrand Russell's "thought for the day":
The good life is inspired by love and guided by knowledge.

If love is the rootage to the tree of life and even its very sap, then the branches of knowledge at their vital tips reveal the ever-moving not quite infinite boundaries of human love— in mathematical jargon, life's *singularity* . . . .

It's worth pondering.

I love philosophy and its analogies but . . .

. . . analogies limp, and the tree of philosophy appears too often leafless. A leafless tree may precede a winter freeze, or it may contain the hope of spring as one sights the first crocus. How shall we work with or from "bare" philosophy?

Before I could type in my answer this morning, I had to rush home for my ever-elusive flash drive, which contains at least two versions of this book. On the way there, I glimpsed a troop of children entering what I took to be their hostess's home. One small child and her accompanying adult were firmly grasping each other's hand.

Wasn't someone in this picture frame "inspired by love" or "guided by knowledge"?

In this connection, a good fried writes, "Russell's quote... reminds me most of a leaf's respiration (inspiration) and DNA's ability to guide an organism's structure."

For me, Russell's statement can also encompass "handclasps" between nature and human life, as well as between love and knowledge.
—WG

23

Love and Indifference
What I Saw in Bombay

The opposite of love is not hate. It is indifference. — Mother Teresa

A certain scene is imprinted on my mind's eye, one I can by no means forget. It is a scene I saw late one night thirty-five years ago in a shopping arcade in Bombay, while on a sea trip to Paris.

Over this city towered the Gate of India built by the English in the colonial period to face the sea. On the main road that came up to the sea, gravely dignified buildings stood side by side. To mitigate the fierce heat of the country's climate, a part of the sidewalk had been covered with an arcade. When we approached the arcade at night, something white could be seen almost burying the road. It was people strewn about in heaps, sleeping. In passing by them, one had to bend this way and that to avoid stepping on them because of the narrowness of the way. You had to walk by as gingerly and quietly as possible. They did not move so much as an inch, and one individual, who was standing and sometimes extending an arm to lean wearily against a post, already seemed too weak to utter the words, "Alms, please."

At that same time I glimpsed through the darkness the eyes of a white-haired old woman. A shudder seized my body. Those eyes *gazed blankly into empty space.* I had never before seen such eyes.

Would hopelessness pressed to the limit produce eyes like this? That was a horrible experience!

I spent my youth in Japan right at the end of World War II. At that time I thought I was seeing the worst human misery imaginable as I viewed whole streets that were now burnt-out fields; we all experienced acute shortages of food and other necessities at that time. Then, in addition, I was moved by the sight of the miserably poor figures I saw in the old fishing village of Aberdeen on the south side of Hong Kong Island. Aberdeen's famed Floating Restaurant no longer ranks with "must-see" sightseeing places.

During earlier days in Aberdeen, hundreds, even thousands, of small boats belonged to people who earned their livelihood on the surface of the dirty waters. Most of these sank in the bay. When I saw one of these craft, I noticed on it a cubicle about the width of the boat; the cubicle was formed by hanging awnings. In it a family lived together and conducted their lives.

Until I saw Bombay I thought these two scenes displayed extreme poverty. I would have asked myself: Don't such scenes represent the very depths of poverty?

However, later I happened to see those absolutely miserable eyes looking into empty space as I was going through the arcade in Bombay. At that moment my thinking changed decisively. To illustrate, in Aberdeen no matter how poor and overworked people are, the life they live, is nevertheless, *human life* – or to put it another way – *life-affirming*. Do they consider themselves as poor as outsiders do? Don't the boat people's children manifest gladness and even glee? They are not unhappy.

When the government built high-rise apartments on the land where it was intended for the boat-people to live and work, within just a few weeks of their removal, they all returned to their former house-boats to pursue their life on the water.

We may infer that, while those who live on the water in Aberdeen seem to be trapped in small, even trifling quarters, they still take pride in their very own world where they can be with their families and live their lives. In that sphere they have freedom. The woman under the arcade in Bombay is not such a person. She has no place to live, nothing to eat. Except for the rags wrapped around her body she owns nothing at all. At this time she really can only wait for someone to give her food or some loose coins. Anyone engaging in this kind of begging has scarcely any energy or spirit left. By daybreak every day several of these unfortunates have died. Even if their bodies have not been removed, the facial expression of their neighbors never changes.

Here is total hopelessness. The words "limit situation," which I associate with Sartre, apply here. The phrase refers to the situation in which one's reason, and even feeling, loses the will to resist or even to care. Don't you think Sartre was describing an abysmal wretchedness that he had personally encountered?

In Calcutta, too, where Mother Teresa worked with people in comparable distress, there was no cure or relief from the pain of the ill ones whom she served. For such people, she only wished to provide a place for the dying that would give human dignity to each individual in their last days. No one should be allowed to die in the street like a stray dog. More specifically, she arranged for dying persons at the end of their unfortunate lives to receive empathetic concern as they were tenderly placed on simple cots. Furthermore, these individuals, as they lay dying, would come to know something of *love*.

Now, to consider a bit more deeply: With regard to human life we may realize that, in the last analysis, a crucial part of what is called the "love of God" is the love of our fellow human beings. No matter how poor a person is in their situation, if he or she finds love there, that person can live meaningfully.

Japan revived quickly from the ruins of war. The urban areas overflowed with wreckage. Nevertheless, with so many people surrounding each returnee, how could human love be lacking all around? When others are around to help sustain us, that isn't the time to mourn the loss of humanity, is it? Even when television presents images from all over the world of millions of suffering people (refugees, etc.), those pictures do not imply, do they, that all these individuals have begun to feel total heartbreak or the acute psychological agony of despair?

In Sanskrit such sorrow and distress are connected directly with the word *karuna*. That's because *karuna* hears voices groaning in agony. The exalted Buddha preached that mercy (*karuna*) is at work whenever we make the pain and suffering of others our own.

Among the sayings of Mother Teresa one above all is unforgettable; it is the one at the head of this Encounter. "The opposite of love is not hate. It is indifference."

Bridge 23

In the above context, the reader will understand that Mother Teresa was not minimizing the destructive power of hatred. Her point, rather, is that the victim of a hateful act has at least some chance to respond humanly to the perpetrator. An indifferent passerby does not evoke any response other than deepening despair, all loss of hope. In a way some relationship – even a bad one – is better than simple indifference and neglect.

Sartre encouraged his readers to be "engaged," that is, to get involved in political action to improve society. . . .

Hattori concurs in this advice, but his next comment reveals that there is an unexpected challenge.

> However, when we saw people *waiting to die* under the arcade in India, what kind of "existential" action to improve society was being asked of us? Mother Teresa's action was more direct, and it was indisputably Christian.

Furthermore, to avoid such actions may imperil our humanity and even our health. "In 1988, Harvard researchers coined the term 'the Mother Teresa effect' to describe how merely watching an act of altruism can be good for you...." (*The Boston Globe*, Feb. 12, 2005, "Dose of spirituality has healthful effect.") My minister, Pastor Phyllis Kumorowski, summarized other good effects in a recent sermon. As I understood her, they included improving the body's defense mechanisms, speeding clotting, and reducing chest pains.

Now I'd like to invite Veronica McAsey, the head librarian at Southwestern College, to join our discussion. Veronica, I believe that you have your own perspective on Mother Teresa as presented by Eiji Hattori.

"Yes, Wallace, I do – two in fact. As a Catholic I can remember first learning about the saints and followers of Christ quite early. They were normal individuals similar to Mother Teresa who heard the call to help those in need. They did not plan to change the world, but their example of service radiated beyond their village, city, or country thus inspiring others. The amazing aspect of service is that it spreads its influence beyond its direct beneficiaries and encourages others not only spiritually but also professionally.

"As a librarian, my chance to call a student's attention to a book such as *Deep Encounters* is gratifying. Even single chapters, like episodes 10 and 23 in which Mother Teresa's dedication and wisdom feature prominently, inspire me to order the book for the library of our small Protestant liberal-arts college."

* * *

Someone skeptical of altruism might object that the moment we begin to speak, or even think, of the health benefits from altruism, it is no longer altruism, because self-interest (in hope of benefits to our own health) has entered the picture. But to appreciate a connection of my health and other blessings with thoughts or acts of mercy is no proof that my concern for the other is not also real and authentic.

A reader might wonder if love is quite enough in facing hopelessness. Perhaps we should describe Mother Teresa's type of love as persistent to the point of "keeping on keeping on." A black father often told his family, that he was "born in a cradle of butcher knives, rocked in a cradle of beehives; rattlesnakes bit me then crawled off and died." The son who reports these words adds, "But I also learned from him . . . that the toughest thing you'll learn in life is persevere. Hold out hope. . . Hold on."[1]

Of course, Hattori is asking about those who can't hold on. . . .

---

1. Mark McCormack, Commentary, *Wichita Eagle*, 4-20-06.

24

Under the Baobab Tree
Reflecting on Democracy

In Africa, according to Henri Lopes, when there are debates between those in the majority and those holding an opposing minority opinion, "It is possible the minority opinion may be the better one."

Ever since the Middle ages Valencia has been a city facing the Mediterranean Sea. I was invited to that city for a big symposium scheduled for January, 1997, with the theme, "The Challenge of the Third Millennium." It was conceived on a grand scale to consider not only the 21st century but the whole next millennium. In addition to the well-known scholars from twenty-seven nations, there were former heads of state, prime ministers, and ministers of state from ten countries as well as representatives of UNESCO, the European Council and the World Bank. The whole assemblage engaged in heated debates for three days.

As the only Japanese delegate, I was impressed by the solid response of the audience to my presentation entitled, "In Search of Common Values in Cultural Diversity." The audience, which filled the hall, consisted mostly of young people.

One impressive thing about this conference was that "compassion" became its key word. Both scholars and statesmen explained the need for the coming millennium to recapture compassion in the human heart and mind, indeed to establish human survival on it. Compassion means *sharing the pain of others* with affection and benevolence. The *market principles* associated with Western liberalism have spread all over the world. A free market economy involves the law of the jungle, the survival of the strong. Furthermore, its motivating energy has been nothing less than desire or Greed.[1] A market economy creates desire even where none existed before and thereby limitlessly increases feelings of dissatisfaction and frustration. For this reason, the population explosion provokes a tenfold explosion of consumption and is tending toward the ruin of our only planet-home.

Such destruction must be prevented. However, for earth and humanity to be saved a new political principle must be found. None of the collapsed forms of *socialism* will help. They ineffectively were brought forward to counter liberalism's exploitative individualism; idealized socialism espoused instead a leveling "equality" or social solidarity. (But efforts to enact the ideal fell far short.)

The people who came together in Valencia from all around the world crafted political and economic principles for the future; they fixed their eyes upon the problem of *kokoro* (the human heart and mind) as it appears of old and as it will continue to challenge future generations.

At this conference the debates of many people – statesmen included – converged on the issue of the Crisis of Democracy. It is not simply a crisis for the so-called developing nations but one faced by more advanced democratic nations as well.

Under present systems of election, persons of broad outlook and long-range perspective are scarcely ever elected. The recently elected member of a diet or congress immediately begins to think about how to garner votes for the next election. And the principle of decision by majority opinion divides winners from losers on margins as slim as 51% to 49%.

On close reflection, it will be realized that at the time of Pericles in Athens where democracy was born, vote counts such as "49% for and 51% against" had never occurred to anyone. A leader directly addressed the people, and when 80% or more all agreed they raised a mighty cheer.[2]

What I'll never forget about this kind of democracy is something told me by Henri Lopes, the former Prime Minister of the Congo and former Assistant

---

1. I thought the British economist E. F. Schumacher coined the aphorism "Greed is good" as a short critique of exploitative capitalism, but I do not find the axiom in his best seller, *Small Is Beautiful* (New York: Harper & Row, 1973). He does use a Buddhist perspective (and to some extent Hindu as well) to critique unlimited desire and thus make the same ironic point as the axiom. Also, the subtitle of his book gives exactly the same emphasis that our author Hattori is presenting: "Economics as if People Mattered."
2. Of course, percentages were not used when Pericles thrived. They help us make our point now. If Shakespeare could put a chiming clock in *Julius Caesar*, we may be allowed a little leeway with our percentages. Besides, the Japanese love them even more than Americans! With 60% probability? – WG

Director General of UNESCO. He said, "In Africa, you see, when a problem arose the village chief gathered all the villagers together under the baobab tree. When those gathered conferred, many persons favored one opinion and a small number opposed it. What do you think the chief does?"

"Isn't the final decision made by the majority in accordance with the democratic principle?" I answered.

Lopes explained, "No, it is not. The African leader thinks like this: 'It is possible the minority opinion is the better one.' Therefore, the meeting under the baobab tree will be closed for that day; it will be reconvened in the same place the next day."

That is surprising, isn't it?

At the beginning of democracy it was important to respect minority opinions. We must recall that from this principle of mutual respect, the dialogues of Socrates were born. Plato in his *Dialogues* depicts the figure of Socrates quite dramatically as a master of learning through dialogue.

Imagine now how the master goes about stimulating profound discussion among his followers. He brings up an opinion that is the opposite of what was originally felt by the majority of his listeners. With great patience he leads the discussion by means of question and metaphor; this enables the audience to see various angles of approach to the riddle posed by opposite ideas. He elucidates various points of view, and ultimately the illuminating discussion resolves the riddle so that its proper solution is found in an opinion contrary to what has been accepted uncritically. And so in the end a resolution is reached that at least tentatively satisfies everyone. It avoids dogmatic certainties that may be premature, wrongheaded, or even dangerous.

We must realize that the spirit shown by Athenian statesmen was energized by these dialogues. This same spirit has mysteriously come to dwell under the baobab tree. At the present time in Japan, matters are beginning to change slightly, but for a long time the Japanese wished to catch up with and even surpass "advanced" Western countries but neglected the cultures that have thrived in Africa and Asia.

Nevertheless, the compassion discussed in Valencia has certainly taken root in Asia and Africa; by contrast, a crisis of democracy is what one sees while visiting the advanced countries.

The world has arrived at a point where dialogue fades away and complex deadlocked issues are sometimes decided and dismissed by a single ballot. Socrates' death is symbolic of the mistakes democracy can make. What made the difference between life or death for him was the color of a few seashell ballots.

Bridge 24

I have been curious about how a political scientist enmeshed in America's "great experiment" with democracy might interpret the baobab process. I cannot speak as such a specialist, but I can imagine from some introductory work in American government classes part of a response, as follows:

In light of the much more formalized American system, we can see that in village governance the "executive officer" is given more flexible veto power than in a much more complicated society. Village democracy entails substantial authority to modify and even cause the group to review or revoke decisions. This system puts less restraint on the chief than on a *chief of state* in a society where laws are intended to prevent arbitrary abuses of power. In short, the chief's words and his work seem to combine in one person what elsewhere evolved into separate and somewhat segregated government branches or bureaucracies. The African village system grants the leader of superior wisdom the opportunity both to lead more creatively and to prevent foolish majority decisions.

Supplemental to such an analysis is Hattori's thoughtful comment above, "Under present systems of election, persons of broad outlook and long-range perspective are scarcely ever elected." Translated into the culture shaded by the baobab tree, the issue becomes, "What if the chief is not wise?"

In his note to Japanese readers, Hattori observes that in the tradition of the baobab tree, "The night brings wisdom when the group's decision is carried over to the next day."

Even in more complex societies, "sleeping on it" helps the final decision to be better considered. But in such societies, pressures other than wisdom are too frequently overpowering.

Hattori manages one more shift of emphasis.

> Now, in all sorts of respects African countries are becoming involved in horrible conditions, but originally these evils were brought on by European colonialism. Pre-colonial Africa did not have these evils. According to Lopes, the Western African tradition was just as I have described it.
>
> When we reflect carefully on the best prospects for the 21st century, we realize that human problems cannot always be solved by passage of laws of more or less unlimited duration.

The brittleness of some American legalistic formulas is one of our concerns here. The antithesis of brittleness shines through a recent Kansas obituary of Mrs. Laura Dobbs (aged 88). We all might metaphorically benefit from gathering under her baobab tree.

The obituary reads, "Almost all her life she nursed and cared for people." She worked. . . .with the poor in Africa, Alaska, and Peru, and served with Mother Teresa in Bombay, India. A mission director who worked with her said, "Wherever we were, she was always talking to people and wanting to know about their culture. I have a wonderful picture of her talking under a tree with a tribal chief. She's showing him a picture of Kansas. She delighted in sitting down with people who were totally different and sharing a part of herself with them." (*The Wichita Eagle*, August 15, 2007).

Political scientist Dr. Gordon Mercer confirms our general approach in this chapter:

> Some important points are made here on minority expression and the importance of dialogue. I fear that we do not see enough dialogue, as this meeting [the 1998 UNESCO symposium] makes apparent. When dealing with majority rights and minority rights I often think of the contradictions in Jean-Jacques Rousseau as he deals with the problems of the general will and who interprets it.[3]

---

3. From personal correspondence from Mercer to Gray.

25

The Tree of Life
Climbing the Symbiotic Line

> In Africa that Tree of Life is remembered with deep feeling. Innumerable human bodies have been carved into one tree trunk to express a life-link, one which continuously persists and climbs from the past to the future.

The word *kyōsei* (symbiosis) is often heard in recent years, but it is a relatively new Japanese word. In 1987 the "philosophy of *kyōsei*" was advocated by the architect Kishō Kurokawa[1], and only about then did the term become widely known and included in Japanese dictionaries.

When we human beings look back upon the scientism that has prevailed since the 17th century dream of totally subduing nature, and when we reflect on modern history, which is constantly littered with nationalistic wars, these developments drive us to recognize the fresh significance of the word *kyōsei* as a new value for the 21st century.

The Japanese word *kyōsei* has no exact translation in the languages of Europe or America. Sometimes it is translated by the English expression "living together." However, even though this translation can express the sense of interracial harmony

---

1. According to the website of Kishō Kurokawa and Associates – accessed on 3/2/2006 at http://www.kisho.co.jp/Company/office-e.html – the company has used this approach to architectural approach to architectural design for "more than 100 projects over the past 40 years."

and cooperation, it does not contain the twin ideas of living together with all living non-human beings and with the natural environment as a whole.

On the other hand, the English word "symbiosis" was already in usage in biology about a century earlier in Europe and America. How about using this word as it is? In fact, I do use it sometimes.

However, the word does not exactly catch the richness and breadth of the word *kyōsei* unless we enlarge the interpretation of the English term. "Symbiosis" in its biological sense deals generally with the relation between two life forms. In contrast to bare parasitism, it refers to mutual benefits shared by a host and its biological "partner."[2] Certain plant organisms such as mistletoe, in order to live on their tree host, cling to it with one-sided dependency. In sharp contrast to these parasites, there are plant bacteria that use the roots of specific trees for themselves but also assist their hosts to live.

Surely *kyōsei*, as the relatively new term for a rather ancient concept, includes the axiom, "By assisting the partner you can keep yourself alive." Yet there is still a problem, for this is limited to only two kinds of living beings.

In contrast to this idea, what we seek when we use this new term, is recognition of the cosmic extent of mutual relationships. Moreover, through reflection on such relationships we may discover that there is in them a secret design for all creation in the *future*! Kurokawa has summarized his own advocacy of symbiosis in five ways:

- *Kyōsei* speaks of opposition and contradiction.
- *Kyōsei* involves our need of each other.
- *Kyōsei* makes possible new acts of creation.
- *Kyōsei* encourages mutual respect, even for each other's sanctuaries, thus enlarging the commonalities.
- *Kyōsei* involves giving and being given to.

In fact, from the same Chinese characters (共生) now usually pronounced *kyōsei*, Kurokawa recalls an old word used in Jōdo, a Buddhist sect that has existed in Japan since the 12th century. As used in Jōdo, the word was pronounced *tomoiki* ("living together"). It implied an ontology,[3] the idea that everything consists of

---

2. I wondered about Hattori's usage here. When I checked the dictionaries, I found that Random House has given a most precise and concise definition, as agreed upon by scholars of the English language. It states that symbiosis refers to "the living together of two dissimilar organisms, especially when this association is mutually beneficial." This definition completely supports Hattori's discussion above. See *The Random House Dictionary of the English Language* (1967).
3. In its basic philosophical sense, "ontology" refers to the cataloguing and discussion of what is thought to exist in the universe and not just in the tangible or physical mode. Philosophers give reasons for their respective lists as well as criticisms of lists they consider too long or too short.

such opposites as life and death, good and evil, light and darkness. Kurokawa's point of departure is acceptance of this thought, a thought that can be retraced to the even older consciousness-only (*vijnapti-matrata*) school formed in the fourth century A.D. This school of Buddhist thought is called *yuishiki* in Japanese, but there are Sanskrit and Chinese precedents for the word.

The *tomoiki* concept has been added to our modern appreciation of originality or creativity. A fully modern, even future version of symbiosis is thus being born. From this perspective, what occurs is the willingness to see all other viewpoints in a way that avoids defiling or contaminating anyone's sanctuary. At the same time, each person will have an attitude of seeking out whatever values may be held in common while preserving one's own distinctive "sacred precincts." Then when common ground is uncovered, the cultivation of it will disclose new approaches for terms such as "creation" or "all creation."

Everything on earth continues to be bound together in mutual relationships, so the philosophy of symbiosis, which recognizes the principle of *being kept alive by mutuality*, is a valuable message for Japan to share with the world. The fact that in many international conferences the word *kyosei* (in Western letters) has begun to be used in just such a way may reflect the spread of that message.

However, something has been missing in discussions of *kyōsei* in Japan until now.[4] It is the vertical line of *kyōsei*.

I remember the deep feeling evoked by the Tree of Life I saw in Africa. It was a tree where innumerable human bodies were carved into the one tree trunk. It expresses a chain that endures forever.

I have seen quite comparable carvings (or totems) in Papua New Guinea. An Indian totem in Canada also has fundamentally the same conception as that carving. The idea of "ancestor worship" is especially obvious in the cultural area of the Pacific. For all those who have a vigorous feeling in daily life that the ancestors watch over us, it follows that we ourselves must also be fully sensitive to the lives of descendants who will "ascend" the vertical line of living together in the future. At a symposium held in Belem, Brazil, I was deeply impressed when a certain African representative said, "We live with the Unborn."

In 1997 Jacques-Yves Cousteau, the great scholar of planet Earth, concluded his life of 87 years by drawing up a petition on the "rights of future generations." For it he gathered nine million signatures. The aim of the petition was to assure that we all might work toward "preserving the beauty of this earth," an earth entrusted to us by future generations. And in the fall of 1997 – Cousteau had died

---

4. The reader will note a slight difference in the representation of the same word in Romanized form: *kyōsei* and *kyosei*. Author Hattori has chosen to omit the bar (macron) from over the word when he writes it in the alphabet familiar to Western readers who may have little knowledge of the Japanese language. For scholars and the Japanese themselves, the length of vowels is critical in distinguishing near homonyms from each other.

in June of that year – the fruit of his work was confirmed at a UNESCO general conference in the form of the resolution adopted by all member states. It was "A Declaration of the Responsibility of the Present Generation for All Future Generations."

The message of *kyōsei* should become a genuine contribution to the future of humanity, when humanity recognizes the vertical line as well as the horizontal breadth of human interactions in the present.

Bridge 25

I see the "tree of life" rising from a single root system with many branches extending shade to a rich variety of forms of life in general and styles of culture in particular

Paraphrasing what I sense Hattori's additional comments to Japanese readers to be intimating, I find him suggesting:

> What is referred to as the "Tree of Life" is a "stream of life" that is, so to speak, "carved" or formed like waves on waves rising from ancestors to descendants, from deep roots to the tips of branches, a flow in which all humanity is joined.
>
> I have a strong impression whenever I reflect on the "stream of life" that it encompasses the as-yet unborn generations, as well as the present and past ones. The Stream of Life that I saw in Tanzania had been carved in a dead tree and was a few meters tall. I was shocked to see that something I regarded at first glance as fit only to become fireplace kindling had instead been shaped into this amazing piece of a nation's memory as well as its dream of the future.
>
> Japanese *symbiotic theorizing* at the present moment is a symbiosis of "width" only, that is, a symbiosis of nature, of neighborliness, and of appreciation of other cultures. It's mainly a matter of *breadth* as regards the chain of life. What is rarely thought of in this country of Japan is the "transportation," if you will, of this concern to future generations. That is the issue to which I have wished to call attention.

Hattori has made me aware for the first time of the full suggestiveness of the "tree of life" metaphor. I had not known of the woodcarving tradition in southern Tanzania by that name. The tradition is somewhat independent of, yet congruent with, both the Biblical image and the Leakeys' work in East Africa. Another collective name for it is "Makonde Carving" because the Makonde people are the ones who produce these carvings.

The website devoted to their work is sustained by the African Blackwood Conservation Project (http://www.blackwoodconservation.org/carving.html). Of this blackwood genre of East African craftsmanship, the website states, "Their work is both traditional and contemporary, reflecting a tribal past as well as modern response to urban life. . . . They utilize their tribal myths and stories as inspiration for the masterful work."

Artist-in-residence Kate Mangold of my hometown, Winfield, Kansas, USA, pointed out to me that instead of a monotonous and stereotypical "standing on the shoulders of preceding generations," these artists have some of the daily *activities* of their extended family resting on the similar activities of those who are contemporary or who have passed on before. According to the website, a six-foot-high carving can represent at least nine-month's labor for the artist.

However, Hattori's major point is that our kind treatment of beautiful earth will assure that our successor will be able not only continue to live but to thrive as well.

26

Stories of Deities[1]
From the Soul of the Ainu People

According to Morio Senke, an Ainu, spruce trees and fir trees are "working" here. However, larch trees do not work in the winter.[2]

In olden times, *yanagi* or willow trees grew in the land of gods. When autumn came, then willow leaves would flutter, dance briefly in the wind, and fall to the ground in Ainu land. The gods took pity on the leaves that soon rotted away so completely; they chose to give them new life as fish. These small silvery fish are now called capelin, a smelt-like fish.

Ainu legends are rich with poetic sentiment. And for long the Ainu have been a kindhearted people living at peace with their gods.

Sometime before 1867/68, which ended the Tokugawa Shogunate and signaled Japan's entry into the modern world, a Japanese explorer visited the land of the Ainu (Ezo, now known as Hokkaido). He made a map and recorded Ainu place names. His name is Matsuura Takeshiro. It is due to him that place names in what is now called Hokkaido are what they are.

The Chinese characters once pronounced Kusuri in Matsuura's "Diary of Kusuri" are today pronounced *Kushiro*. We also understand that this last is

---

1. *Kamui-yukar*、カムイ ユーカラ.
2. A handwritten note by the author explains, "The Ainu people think all living beings WORK for others, like humans."

identical to what is generally known as Lake Kuccharo. Even in modern Japan almost all places in Hokkaido are known by their Ainu names.

What is remarkable about the accomplishments of Matsuura Takeshiro is that they shed light for the study of early Ainu-land (Ezo-chi). He became a friend of these native people, learned their language and even received cooperation from the Ainu themselves for his survey. What the names generally show is how such diverse peoples can work together with mutual respect. This is quite a different way of proceeding from that employed by some of the first European pioneers in America. They referred to the previous inhabitants as "Indians" because they mistook this continent for India. Then stage by stage they drove the natives farther and farther west, and continued to impose such European names as *New York*, *New Orleans*, *St. Louis*, etc.[3]

Of course, in Japan, too, there was the despotic rule of Matsumae the Lord of northern Honshu and the murder of Shakushain who stood up to oppression by leading the Ainu rebellion of 1669. Only yesterday some of the oppressive laws supposed to "protect" the Ainu were at last lifted.

All these matters should occasion deep reflection. At least there is some solace for our minds in the Ainu place names found everywhere in Hokkaido, and those names serve as a matter of pride in relation to the peoples of the world. This continuing use of earlier place names shows respect for "native Japanese" in their own right. And in Matsuura's "Diary of Kusuri" we find him emphasizing their respect for all creatures: "*So that birds and animals do not flee into the mountains we ought to walk calmly, quietly.*"

Matsuura's consideration for the Ainu people and their ancient culture is evident in his presentation of gifts to each of his Ainu guides and his praying to the tutelary god of Lake Akan for their peace and safety. The history of Hokkaido during the almost 140-year period since the 1860s is labeled the *Clearing*, which means the opening or exploitation (exploitation of land that was "new" only to explorers, conquerors or governmental representatives). If Matsuura Takeshiro had never lived, I think the history of the Clearing would have presented an entirely different and sadder aspect to the world.

A few years ago in the spring, I finally visited a swampland near Kushiro. It is the home of the Red Crowned Crane (*tancho* in Japanese), revered by the Ainu as the God of the Marsh. It is a name that seems nobly suited to this bird and the marsh. In the Ainu language it is pronounced *sarorun kamui*. At that time I saw several old friends who came to see me from the village of Kotan (an Ainu village).

---

3. These facts are mitigated a bit by American pride in names and cultures antedating Columbus. Examples from just the U. S: Chicago; Ponca City, Oklahoma; and Wichita, Kansas. The United Church of Christ even owns a church camp in Idaho named N-sid-sen meaning Point of Inspiration.

In 1976, I opened the first-ever festival of Japanese culture to be held at UNESCO headquarters in Paris. And I invited the Yukara-za, a theater group of Ainu people. The event was held because of my belief that, for the promotion of minority cultures, a power to introduce these cultures on a world stage exists in ways that transcend language barriers. We were thinking of both handcrafted works of art and the ancient Ainu legends and folktales so faithfully passed down by generations of storyteller clans.

Through many centuries the "Yūkara" were epic songs or poems which conveyed from father to son the Ainu traditions. But nobody now can understand these narratives when pronounced in the archaic fashion. In the Yukara theater-form created by young Ainu, the tradition took on a fresh visual aspect.

Kamui Yūkara is an account of the world's creation. During the Yukara Company's performance under director Toko Nuburi, our spirits were united from the very beginning of the program in the stage wings, even before the raising of the curtain. What we saw and heard was a ceremony called *Kamui Nomi*, prayer to gods of the land. While the drama was under way, the silence in the auditorium became profound and the tension high. The clapping afterwards was thunderous; it engulfed the house with waves of spirited response. In a moment of deep and lasting emotion, the heart of the Ainu people linked itself to the people of the world.

Like the Alaskan name "Innuit" (Eskimo), the word "Ainu" signifies "human being." It became an ethnic name only after the arrival of the Japanese or *Wajin*. All these groups are in a symbiotic relationship with Mother Nature; they see their gods in nature. Moreover, their gods are so human that they gather for recreation in Kamui Mintara (the garden for gods at play). While gods should be treated with honor and reverence, aren't there lighter times when, like equals, they are asked, "Aren't you gods awful, too"? The *charanke* in Ainu means a quarrel with the gods. The Ainu killed game only as necessary to sustain human life, so before a kill was consumed as food, appreciation was expressed to the god-animal and an arrow shot heavenward to send the animal's spirit back. The festival in Japanese is *Kuma Matsuri* (the Bear Festival), but the exact meaning of the Ainu name *Iomante* is, "The Return of the Bear."

Waves of modernization have succeeded in smashing or overwhelming such ethnic groups. Especially after the Meiji Era, the policy of assimilation robbed the Ainu of the language by which they might express their soul and spirit. "Civilization" rushed into the vacuum and completely filled it, not only with such things as cars and electricity but with materialistic attitudes as well.

What the guide, Mr. Morio Senke, said, as we proceeded toward Akan National Park, has lodged itself in my brain. According to him, "spruce trees and fir trees are working here. However, larch trees do *not* work in the winter." The *kasamatsu* (larch trees), brought here by the Japanese, lose their leaves in winter in order to hibernate . . . . I know also that these people living at the Akan lakeside can communicate with the people of the world even more than ordinary Japanese.

Put another way, the Ainu feel that the trees introduced by the Japanese drop their leaves for the same reason that rivers shrink during what they call "winter's sleep." In addition to the poetic overtones of the guide's remarks, there is the clear suggestion that the native fir and spruce trees that continue to "work" in winter are a better ecological fit for Hokkaido than the imported Japanese larch.

Now, the primordial forest of Shiretoko (in Ainu, "at the ends of the earth") must be protected and preserved. That forest affords the last habitable space for the Owl, the god protecting the villages of the Ainu.

Bridge 26

This encounter is an important instance of what happens when peoples migrate, invade, cooperate, dominate, decimate, intermarry or otherwise "mix." The positive and negative aspects of such events in Japan have important parallels, echoes, and impacts all over the world.

Languages change or vanish. Pioneer choices of proper names can reflect disregard for native tradition, even contempt for it. On the other hand, adaptation of native ways and words reflects at least subliminal respect and appreciation...

In a note to me, author Hattori has written, "Now, in Japan most Ainus are married to Japanese to such an extent that there are no more pure Ainu. Historically all four islands of Japan have been inhabited by Ainu."

For an ethnic group to completely lose its linguistic identity is, for Hattori, equivalent to losing its very soul. However, the most creative peoples, including the Japanese, have greatly benefited from their "mixed" inheritances both in the genetic and cultural sense, and an assimilated group may enjoy a significantly enlarged "soul."

Ainu performers have a way of preserving important aspects of their language and culture. Hattori explains how.

> In the oral transmission of stories there is always the fear that something may be lost or changed over long periods of time. However, that worry for anyone who has seen the Yukara company on stage, is quickly recognized as unnecessary.
>
> The Yukara storyteller hits the front of the fireplace with a baton or beater as he sings, thus making a slow rhythm for the story's melody to be sung in an easy yet stately manner. If the language is changed even a little, the rhythm is thrown completely off; it fluctuates and almost goes crazy. This is a clear signal that some of the wording has been changed and needs to be restored to its correct form. Words, the meaning of which is no longer understood, have nevertheless been passed down intact. In the rhythm of the performance the audience feels an uncanny and overwhelming power that leaves deep and lasting impressions.

27

The Tragedy of Easter Island
A Warning from Jacques Cousteau

We must recognize that the largest water reservoir is a forest, not one made by a dam. In Easter Island, due to the *stripping of trees* from the land, the ecosystem has collapsed and the sea around it has also died.

That was what began on Easter Day, 1722. On that day a Dutch explorer discovered a mysterious solitary island in the South Pacific.[1] It was a naked island without any trees; it was stripped even of palms trees, indispensable for any island in a southern seas. Before this particular island was discovered by Westerners, its previous inhabitants knew it as Rapa Nui. It was baptized Easter Island for the date of its discovery.

On this island where only several hundred people were living quite simply, the Dutch nevertheless saw astounding things. Many stone statues of mysterious appearance reach heights of even six to eight meters. These *moai*, as they are called, have been found lying along the coast just as they fell. All have huge

---

1. The Dutch explorer, Jacob Roggeveen, was the discoverer. He "found the island [and] named it for the holy day." – "A Short Prehistory and History of Easter Island." http://islandheritage.org/eihistory.html. (No author listed.) All text and photos on this site © 2001 Easter Island Foundation. All rights reserved. Accessed 7-13-06. Actually, degradation began before European contact. Concerning some recent discoveries and conclusions about this, consult the chapter "Twilight at Easter" (79-119) in Jared

heads, short bodies, and vacant eyes. For two centuries there has been discussion as to why these huge sculptures happened to appear on such a solitary island. Also debated was what kind of history the island hides.

The Norwegian Thor Heyerdahl in 1953 reached this island from Chile on the famous Kon-Tiki raft.; at that time he thought Easter Island culture had its origins in an ancient civilization of South America such as that of the Incas. For example, he proposed that the Eastern Islanders borrowed knowledge and skills from the Incas' massive stonework architecture. Nowadays nobody believes that hypothesis. These early Easter Islanders came from Polynesia.

To be specific, their point of origin in about the third century is the Marquesas Islands.[2] The Polynesian seafarers par excellence began to build and sail larger ships for more extensive navigation, a practice that continued until more recent times. They were looking beyond boundless waves toward new islands and did not hesitate to cross vast oceans to touch land there. One of their boats must have drifted ashore on Easter Island.[3] This is why *moai* also embody the spirits of the ancestors as in other Polynesian islands; among those islands there remain the sanctuaries called *ahu*, which in Tahiti are known as *marae*.

There must have been less than a hundred voyagers who went ashore in those first landings. The residential population of Easter Island seems also to have increased to around 20,000 in the 17th century. This shows that the island was endowed with the right conditions to sustain life. So what caused the sharp decrease which follows? Why does the whole island appear in such a ruined condition? It is a fact that in the 18th century, half of the then-surviving residents were led away into slavery in South America. But this happened when life on this island had already been threatened and was beginning to collapse.

Residents were divided between a "long-eared tribe" and a "short-eared tribe." Those two tribes began to war with each other. They killed each other's priests and proceeded to pull down the other side's *moai* statues, their tutelary deities.

Diamond's *Collapse: How Societies Choose to Fail or Succeed* (Viking, 2005). For "Further Readings" and supportive data, consult pp. 531-534 of *Collapse*. Since the publication of "Deep Encounter" in its Japanese version (1999) many refinements of the complicated story of Easter Island have emerged, but on the major thesis of Hattori and Jacques Cousteau that this remote island is a metaphor of what will happen to planet earth if we don't wake up and take proper measures, *Collapse 118-119* is in absolute agreement.

2. For an update from scientific work since 1999, consult *Collapse* (88) where it is reported that attention now shifts to Mangareva, Pitcairn, and Henderson.
3. Diamond (88) suggests that Polynesian navigational strategies may have been much better than previously supposed so the voyagers may have used their sighting of flocks of birds foraging a hundred miles from Easter Island to zero-in on the island. This would take some the happenstance out of their discovery.

But on an island that had enjoyed at least a thousand years of peace, why did war break out in the late 17th or early 18th century? Answer: Because the island became destitute. In fact, food vanished. *Well, why did food vanish?* This is the most important question. The answer is, *"Because they cut down the trees."*

At one time this island, like all the islands of the South Pacific, must have had forests. The residences for 20,000 people, the ships, the *ahu* shrines, the tools, ropes[4] and devices for building and transporting *moai* – all these required wood. Now Easter Island is denuded and treeless. When rain flows over treeless land in one breath and departs in the next, people cannot even farm.

We must recognize that the largest water reservoir is not one made by a dam but, rather, it's a forest. We must also understand forests and their role. Tree roots take in and hold water; they make rivers.[5] The microorganisms that grow in forests nourish other aquatic microorganisms in the rivers. These microorganisms in turn nourish small fish. That bio-rich water pours into the sea. The sea also hosts and brings forth an abundance of living things. A proverb says, "To get a fish you must plant a tree." Due to the stripping of trees from Easter Island the eco-cycle was interrupted resulting in the death also of the surrounding ocean. That led naturally to shortages, which in turn resulted in humans slaughtering each other and accelerating their ruin of the environment. Since we are in partnership with all forms of life we must abandon any delusions about escaping our environment; human beings cannot live outside the ecosystem.

After his invention more than sixty years ago of the aqualung for scuba diving, Jacques Cousteau opened the mysteries of the ocean floor before our eyes with the warning, "If humankind does not change the way it is walking, it will suffer the same fate as Easter Island."

What we have seen in the downfall of many ancient civilizations teaches us the same lesson. Mycenae (the Aegean Sea civilization), Mohenjodaro (an Indus River civilization), and Ephesus (a center of Greek civilization) all perished by cutting down their trees. Will we modern people avoid committing the same error on a global scale? By the turn of the 21st century, we had already lost half the tropical rain forests of the world.

Easter Island is listed as a World Heritage site by UNESCO and, through the precedent-setting cooperation of Japan and a number of other nations, *moai* statues are again standing upright in rows. The huge images, their eyes of white coral and black obsidian reinserted in the sockets to restore their original form, are facing inland, still watching over their villages. However, we must not forget

---

4. According to Diamond (102), the "long, thick ropes [were made] from fibrous tree bark."
5. "Water transpiration from trees returns water to the atmosphere, so that deforestation tends to cause diminished rainfall and increased desertification. Trees retain water in the soil and keep it moist. . . . Some forests . . . hold the major portion of the ecosystem's nutrients. . . ." Diamond 469.

what these eyes have looked upon. They saw how from ignorance the village's own people were driven into the situation of a final desperate war. An islander's picture carved on a coastal cliff shows the people at their final prayers on an island of no more boats. "I want to be a bird and go somewhere!"

If someone is a bird from Easter Island and flies a great distance, then such a bird may at last find somewhere to land. However, no bird can escape this earth.[6]

Bridge 27

My footnotes updating the best recent research on the Easter Island's complex history do not diminish the warning it sounds for Earth's possible collapse. Hattori, Cousteau, and Diamond are clear on that point, but it may elude some readers. After Easter's discovery by its pre-European inhabitants, no outside enemy caused the inhabitants to abuse their limited resources. They continued unassisted on their creep toward ecological, political and religious disaster.

In the note to Japanese readers of Chapter 27, Hattori elaborates on Cousteau's contributions to global ecology through the book and movie *Silent World* and the ABC TV series on Worlds Rediscovered. For example, one segment of the series introduces us to a different perspective on major rivers of the world.

One startling fact might be added to buttress Hattori's ecological argument. During a particularly repressive occupation of the island, 70,000 sheep were added to an already overstressed environment. As was to be expected, they further denuded the island. For details see *Collapse* 112. Somewhere Hattori has said something like this:

"What we are required to do now is to become truly civilized. A civilized person is one who knows oneself and tries to learn from others and from nature. Our future must be based on the spirit of *mutual respect*, on the very *wisdom* of knowing that mutual respect does lead to *mutual benefit*."

My friend Wes Jackson is the founder of the Land Institute headquartered in Salina, Kansas, USA. Recently in The Land's newsletter he has asked readers to "look at the four forms of capital that economists describe: natural, built, social and human. Land, water, air, forests and soils are natural capital. . . . Human capital is our activity, our creativity. The challenge is to redirect our *social* and *human* capital toward tool making, tool use and "built" environment that draws on the earth's natural capital at no more than its rate of replacement." Jackson feels as Cousteau, Hattori and I do that science can help us interact with our environment wisely, that is, not ruining it but even enhancing its beauty and habitability.

---

6. Even a spacecraft that leaves earth must have on board some important parts of earth's environment and restock air, food, water and other essentials from time to time. Otherwise, the craft and its astronauts will perish.

28

Churning the Sea of Milk
Decline and Creation

I see this myth as a picture of a creative process reversing human decline. It is a warning against the tendency of human life to fall into inertia. Keeping the status quo is like letting water stagnate. So far as human life is concerned, "status quo" is already "decline," or, one might say, "the fall of man."

> Souring Milk or Generative Semen?
> – W.G.'s Question
>
> The rotation of the tower-mountain releases a seminal fluid that creates a divine ambrosia . . . . (Michael Buckley)
>
> Hattori's first sentence about creativity is the "point" of the essay. Stay with us on some of the archaeological and mythological details. They may lead to an "Aha!" moment when the point explodes into a star.
> Details and interpretations vary from time to time, culture to culture and person to person. As regards the present chapter, my struggle as translator and Hattori's as interpreter created an arduous self- and other-disciplining.
> The process is, in fact, a large part of the point.

The Kymer Dynasty, which flourished in the 12th century, birthed a gorgeous civilization on the banks of Cambodia's Tonle Sap (Great Lake). Its many huge temples remain until this very day. Among them, Angkor Wat, said to have been built there as his own tomb by Suryavarman II in the 12th century, is a grand pyramidal shaped temple; the circumference of the outer wall is almost six kilometers. It consists of three levels, at the center of which five towers imitate Mount Sumeru, the dwelling of the god Indra. There are three sets of corridors, and each set forms a square on its level. The central court on the upper stage (the hanging court) was once a reservoir-pool; the pool area still demonstrates the lovely craftsmanship of the masons. Historically, water flowing down from that area fed the middle-stage pond and then moistened the surface of the earth until at last it reached the outer moat.[1] Angkor was the water-city of the Khmer Dynasty that had founded a nation by means of irrigation. This dynasty's economy was based on agriculture and fishing. Farming could thrive only by means of successful irrigation.

We can imagine how things once looked from the Chinese envoy Zhou Daguan who described the towers as gold-gilded and took a far-reaching perspective on what he observed in the land during his 13th century visit. Just as the towers were golden so were the kings who wore golden costumes. The sun and moon must have lit up the golden towers and golden kings.

Morimoto Ukondayu, a Japanese envoy who in the 17th century left calligraphic graffiti here in Chinese ink, believed it still glorious in the fourteenth, though it was already abandoned at that time. That was because he was so impressed by it in his own later time. He even believed that Angkor Wat was Jitavana Vihara, Buddha's main monastery where he had lived and preached. An understandable error of time and place! It must have seemed like a paradise on earth.

Innumerable smiling goddesses (devatas) and graceful maidens (Apsaras, the only ones who have wings to really fly) are shown floating about. However, let us now attend to the wall of the first corridor on the ground floor. There one may view wonderful carvings on the four faces that extend for 760 meters around the square formed by the ground-floor corridor. This whole array displays legends of the multitudinous Indian gods, principally as they manifest the many aspects of Vishnu. Accompanying these pictorial legends is a representation of the brilliant career of Suryavarman II. And on the southern end of the eastern side there is

---

1. To help visualize and understand the description here the reader may wish to check a website on Angkor Wat, such as http://www.greatbuildings/Angkor_Wat.html. Among other things, websites provide titles of valuable and authoritative reference books. A notable example is Eleanor Mannikka's *Angkor Wat: Time, Space, and Kingship* (Honolulu: University of Hawai'i Press, 1996). I found especially suggestive the sentence concerning the central tower (p. 236), "The apex of the tower points to the formless realm of the gods, far above us in space."

something that everyone must notice. It is a remarkable panel displaying a group of images called, "Churning the Sea of Milk."[2]

The myth recorded in the ancient Indian epic poem of the Mahabharata uses metaphor and allegory to explain the marvelous secret of the destruction and renewal of life and the universe.

In those long-ago days the gods, wanting to obtain the elixir *amrita* of perpetual youth and immortality, consulted with the Asuras (divine beings, spirits, or minor deities). Then the gods gave Mount Mandara a "lift" (because it was sinking into the soft ocean bottom) on the back of the Great Tortoise Kurma or Koorm, an incarnation of the god Vishnu. The great five-headed Serpent Vasuki was coiled around the sacred mountain completely encircling the tower that represents the mountain. The Asuras and gods pulled hard in a gigantic tug-of-war on the serpent's extremities. (Asuras pulled on the heads and Devas on the tail.) On the left or head-side of the serpent there are 96 Asuras, and on the right or tail-side there are 88 deities (*Devas*, Hindu good spirits) who, while tightly grasping it, strenuously tug at the great serpent. In the sky the *apsaras* or celestial spirits[3] dance in celebration of that scene. The flying maidens make music, while beneath them are those who are tugging against each other as they wriggle and sway through innumerable lives.

A central, exceptionally large seated figure is supervising the cosmic game. He is none other than Vishnu, the great god who sustains and governs heaven and earth, indeed life itself.

When the Serpent, who is wound about Mount Mandara, is tugged back and forth from both ends, the mountain creaks and turns right and left. This action stirs the sea so that fish swimming nearby are torn to bits by the violent disturbance. Also, the sea turns the color of milk. It is said that thus it continued for a thousand years. However, finally, by this churning action the sea is able to give birth to the sun and moon, as well as to Śri, a beautiful woman clad in white. This goddess, who is evocative of Venus, soon became Vishnu's wife Lakshmi, the goddess of fortune. With her appearance, the tales tell us, prosperity came back to the world of the gods.

A fantastic story! To me it seems to explain vividly the mystery of life. Marvelous is the thought that a stirred ocean is the mother of life.

---

2. One detail in some of the accounts may explain the double significance of this churning or stirring. By a stirring action, various treasures including the elixir of youth and immortality were lost to the gods and the cosmos. But the churning caused by the cosmic Tug of War also helped in the recovery of these treasures.
3. According to Mannikka, 15, the *apsaras* (often printed as Apsaras) are a Khmer invention. Hattori points out in a note that, while this is true as to their *form*, flying maidens are seen in the renowned Dung Huang Caves and elsewhere since early times. Some say there is a linkage between "Apsaras" and "Angels."

In French we call still water *eau mort* (dead water) and running water *eau vive* (living water). Arthur Rimbaud in his poem *"Aube"* (dawn) writes, "The water was dead," meaning it was calm without any movement. His words, we notice, transmit not only his feeling but a fact. Water will stagnate and die when it does not move. In contrast, a current of limpid water kills bacteria and supports useful life.

That exquisite Indian poem the Mahabharata never fails to impress us with its incorporation of some of the most interesting philosophical principles of nature. The great disturbance of the sea destroys a portion of life (nearby fish, for example). However, in the midst of all this activity, new life flows from the creative process. That is the work of Vishnu, god of preservation and evolution. Western scholars tend to see the Asuras as evil and interpret the scene as the struggle between good and evil. But I do not think so. The concept of an Asura originated in Persia as "Ahura." In India they meet the local gods, Devas. The old gods, Asuras, cooperate with the native ones to create new life. Also, in cooperation with the Persian gods, the Indian ones are searching for eternal life. If we look at the images carefully, we'll discover, right in the midst of the Indian devas, one who sports a Persian hairstyle!

I see this myth as a picture of the decline and re-creation of humanity. It is a warning to humans who tend to be lazy. Preserving the status quo may simply let water stagnate. Totally becalmed waters may signal a decline that has already set in. Compare this to the airplane with a stalled engine. The road to the future is a daily discipline of heart and mind. Nature hands us this lesson..

For several decades Japan has enjoyed an "easy peace" – a kind of a languid feeling induced by too many peaceful days. Now may be a time for stirring. The old gods (government officials) and the new gods (private individuals) might try a tug of war to churn up the ocean a bit.

Bridge 28

Did the attack of 9-11 start the "turning of the churn" once more?

* * *

In his Japanese Note Hattori further illuminates this wondrous temple:

> Angkor Wat is a Hindu rather than Buddhist temple except for the time when Buddhism prospered. Since the temple was originally Hindu, all murals beginning with the first gallery treat Hindu tales.
> The same name "Angkor" attaches to a district in Cambodia where hundreds of Buddhist temples are centered. It spreads out over a rather large area in the hilly part of Cambodia . . . .

Cambodia has clearly distinct wet and dry seasons and can store as little water in the wet season as less than .03 of an inch for use in the dry season. Angkor Wat itself is also dry today, but the pool-shaped terrace in the upper part of the building is suited to catch and hold rainwater. It may even be said that what the Khmer Dynasty symbolized was an irrigation kingdom or even a "water kingdom."

It is thought that the Dynasty was in decline as soon as its irrigation system ceased to function.

29

Land of Gods in the Himalayas
Finding Unexpected Angels Deep in the Mountains

The *dzong* of Tibetan (Tantric) Buddhism is a castle-temple complex devoted to fighting evil spirits. Strangely, the same conception was sketched out by medieval theologians of the West, who referred to a "City of God."

Bhutan is a Shangri-La nestled in the embrace of the Himalayas. People there are gentle, affectionate, and in looks resemble Japanese. The west side of Bhutan contains the Paro Valley with its mountain pass into Tibet. In that pass one finds the Kechurakan Temple that is spoken of as the oldest temple of the country. The building has been rebuilt many times, but in its foundation there remains a stone basement said to date back to the 7th century AD. Crammed in it are many strange images that look like carvings seen in Sri Lanka. When I looked intently at this assemblage I could not believe my eyes. Surprise! Some forms among the images were *angels*. These angels are definitely sprouting wings from their shoulders, but in this period archeologists have not turned up angel-like images anywhere else in Asia. This evoked from me a brusque, "What! You can't be *here!*" My thought was that I was seeing an absolute anomaly for this area.

Those who visit this almost unknown land will be so impressed that time will stop for them. In the high places, as well as in the valleys, banners are lined up like trees in a wooded area. In such places prayerful sutras are being constantly carried by the winds to heaven. There are also *mani* wheels, and at the temple there are similar but larger ones that are waiting to be spun by hand. When devotees circle the temple, walking round and round it, the sutra they dedicate themselves to repeating is *Om Mani Padme Hum*, "Hail, the jewel of the Lotus, hail." With its rapid rhythm, the prayer wheel can emit the mantra (= "sound of truth") more rapidly than any devotee ever could. (River water can also turn a prayer wheel.) The Om Mani is like a beneficent perfume released into the cosmic atmosphere.

The main part of the grand Tibetan complex in Bhutan is a castle called Tashicho Dzong, which is surrounded by mountains. This castle also serves as a Buddhist temple. Its shape tells us how the importation of Tibetan Buddhism affected architecture in Bhutan. It resembles the Potala Palace in Tibet, where one may see the Dalai Lama's historic residence in Lhasa. By design it symbolizes Mount Potala where Kanzeon (also spelled Kannon[1]) resides, but the Dzong of Bhutan unites its own distinctive elegance and flavor with that of its Tibetan prototype.

In an 8th century Tibetan esoteric transmission, there is described a time when the saint Padomasambhava flew over the earth riding a tiger. This monk, who afterwards became revered as Guru Rinpoche ("Precious Master"), founded the Takushan Monastery (The Tiger's Den). To the monastery, which is sort of "pasted" onto a cliff, the practitioners of Buddhist austerities are even today sent to spend an absolutely isolated life.

Many pictures have been painted of all the arhats (perfected Buddhist saints) and dzongs; also the form of the universe has been symbolized in mandalas (meditative diagrams), which have a unique ambiance. Attracting special attention in these pictures are the time wheels (*kalachakras*) that revolve in complex patterns relative to each other, resembling planets circling the earth. This kind of mandala belongs to the tantric school of esoteric Buddhism. If this had been shown me as modern art, I certainly would have accepted the description.[2] In the mandalas each color has its own meaning. So green is earth; blue, water; red, fire; yellow, wind; and white, sky.

There was a pure and bewitching place where I once stood quite still. . . . Something about that place has suddenly come alive in my heretofore blank mind; it concerns an incident that happened 30 years ago in an old castle of the region of Savoie (Savoy) near the French Alps. On that occasion I discovered a certain book.

Generation after generation of the nobility of the Menthon family had inhabited that castle. Once in the summertime I was invited to visit the castle by a descendent, a friend of mine from the University of Paris where we were both students. One day I discovered the book as I browsed the shelves of the

---

1. Avalokiteśvara (Sanskrit) is the bodhisattva who embodies absolute compassion – or, in Hattori's words: "the Deity of Mercy."
2. Hattori also agrees with my angle on this, which I e-mailed him: "This kind of representation must be quite similar to our modern tendency to present the cosmos in abstract pictures or images." – WG

old-fashioned library. It was a 15th century hand-inscribed sheepskin manuscript. Written in Latin, the first letter of every chapter was beautifully decorated. Moreover, here and there brilliantly colored miniature pictures illustrated the text. And the title on the cover stood out in gold letters, St. Augustine's *Civitas Dei* (*The City of God*). The impression it made was unforgettable. Until this time I had understood the "Kingdom of God" to be a transcendent world. However, the illustrations for this book definitely show us its form just as medieval theologians imagined and depicted it. It was a *civitas* or city-state. The people who lived in such a city of God fought in the same way against the city of Satan as they did against other more ordinary castle kingdoms.

That's it. The Bhutanese dzongs constitute the "City of God"!

My thinking on this has gradually clarified so that now I perceive a resonance between such places and the universe we live in. A dzong echoes with sonorous sounds of horns and bass voices chanting Buddhist sutras. All this is joined to the rhythms the drums make. Young priests play instruments made from skulls. Their space invites me quite naturally to take the ultimate prayer posture of throwing myself to the earth.[3]

Perhaps one is permitted to wonder whether what Toynbee celebrated as an advanced or ultimate stage in the development of civilization was not actually this same "City of God." However, such a City of God was not a thousand years of peaceful bliss or supreme goodness but rather any land or city that is always struggling against evil. And, while such a "kingdom" will fight unremittingly against *selfishness*, its central locale is wherever there is a change-over to the *love of God*.[4] It is also true that the *holy* manifests itself in the midst of the mundane and earthy – or even the vulgar.[5] Therefore, as in Japan, one can even find the union of the perfectly sacred with the crudely angry or funny in the Temple of the Great Stupa (a revered grave, with a distinctive shape).

---

3. When my wife and I recently visited Tibet we found it striking how vigorously Buddhist devotees prostrated themselves. Hattori's use of the word "throwing" reminds me of the guide's comment that this exercise can be either for physical health or spiritual discipline/discovery. Long pilgrimages are undertaken by such throwing of oneself forward quickly and repeatedly! If this is "natural," it is the naturalness of the well-trained, deeply committed athlete. But Hattori is recalling the spontaneity of one's *first* prostration.
4. The Japanese *kami no ai* contains the same ambiguity as its English translation, "love of God." It can mean love for God or God's kind of love as expressed toward us. In the present context, the phrase has both meanings, and naturally includes the challenge to love each other as God loves us.
5. In a note to me Hattori says "you can see awful statues of union of male and female gods. Their faces are not of joy but anger. Surrounded by skulls, they are fighting against the evil spirits."

In Bhutan, a land of no graves, in a country that has combined the ways of thinking found in shamanistic Buddhism with the ancient Hindu belief in the transmigration of the soul, there has emerged what we Japanese call *Shingon* (meaning mantra or sacred sound), a form of Buddhism in which both present-day and earlier devotees conduct a prayerful search with all their hearts for the Pure Land. This search even includes scaling peak after peak in the Himalayas.

> ### A Land of No Graves?
>
> If you believe in reincarnation, you do not need graves, for you are always alive somewhere – in some kind of new body. You don't have to wait for the Resurrection of the Dead.

The angels that had changed their form in every Asian country to become heavenly maidens or *apsarases*, may have flitted about from the West until they came to this land where they heard the prayers of the Bhutanese people.

Bridge 29

The Potala is mountain-high while the Tashicho Dzong is in a mountain valley; because of historic isolation, we may envision either Tibet or Bhutan, "as an archetype for the famed Shangri-la."

Here I would like to paraphrase Hattori's Note to his Japanese readers.

> Bhutan shares with other areas a version of Esoteric Buddhism. If you add the original shamanism to Mahayana Buddhism it becomes Tibetan Lamaism (Tantric Buddhism). In addition to its palaces and temples, Bhutan even has a City of God (Buddha land) or city-state with a stronghold or citadel for its citizenry. God (Buddha) even uses weapons besides the diamond pestle and continues to struggle with demons, devils, and Satan. Good and evil spirits are always at each other's throats.

I take this as a metaphor for contending, struggling to the death, with all that is selfish and lacking in compassion. Although all religions have manifested some capacity for violence, it is beyond my capacity to envision any gentle follower of the Buddha as bloodthirsty, though some esoteric pictures and statues look that way.

In a note to me, Hattori made things much plainer for Americans:

> "Bhutanese Buddhists engage in an inner fight against selfishness. Some American Presidents seem to be fighting an outward battle against what they call evil. Perhaps they, like the rest of us, need to fight the *inner fight* to reach the City of God!"

To the Japanese he simply said:

Therefore, contrary to kami (God) or hotoke (the Buddha, or a saint), as conceived in Japan, the divine is not simply perfect completeness. An exasperated, angry or furious visage may be seen in some Buddhist representations. Even monks or priests as servants of God also show this same capacity for deep, unexpected emotionality. They may generally avoid contact with the outside world, confining themselves to their sacred "castles" or spiritual citadels, but they live their whole lives struggling against evil spirits both "out there" in the world and "in here" in the monkish community. Such struggle must continue in every human soul until it is fully enlightened or transfigured. Saints emerge in the process of being diligent in "mortal moral combat" . . . .

Angelic flying beings, as one might expect, probably originated in the Middle East. An image of a "holy spirit that flew" already existed in Assyrian times. I also consider the Greek Eros (Cupid) to be a source for these heavenly beings.

Waves make possible radio and television transmission. They constitute the sounds of music, human conversation, and the chirping of insects, the songs of birds, and "talk" of the higher primates. The colors we see are related to the dynamics of the flow of waves through space. Waves, I believe, even explain much about the chemicals we use and the rocks we study and with which we build. All these kinds of waves have varying frequencies like Tibetan chants. The degrees of abstraction and the choices of metaphor vary between the mandalas or chants Hattori describes and what a physicist theorizes about, but in both approaches the simple contains the "complex" and the complex, the simple.

I want to reiterate what is perhaps the most climactic thought in Hattori's entire presentation: "While such a kingdom will fight unremittingly against *selfishness*, its central locale is wherever there is a changeover to the *love of God*."

30

Black Skies
An Unexpected Attack from Yellow Sands

"There are no birds flying above or beasts walking below." At the end of the 4th century the Buddhist monk Hokken (法顕 Fa Tien in Chinese), who went on a quest for sutras, used this sentence to deplore what he saw in the vast desert of Taklimakan. That desert stretched endlessly along the road he had taken from Dunhuang to his destination as far west as Gandhara.

In the Uigur language Taklimakan means Desert of Death. "Once a man goes into it he never comes out." Both the northern mountain range Tien Shan and the southern range of Kunlun are snow-covered. Even in the West the Pamir Plateau attains a height of 4,000 meters. This space between ranges does its best to cover the center of the vast Tarim Basin with sheer emptiness; it is today the Xinjiang (Sinkian) region in northwest China that in ancient times was regarded by Chinese as the West Area, with no clearly delineated boundary. In the Tang era (618-907) the poet Wang Wei (王維) composed a poem. In it he said, "Once I pass the Yang Gate there will be nobody I know."[1]

The Yang Gate is situated to the southwest of Dunhuang. Along with the Jade Gate in the north, it marks the location where the monks of Tang took their first step in the endless journey across the Desert of Death to search out precious sutras in the far away country of Buddha. Before them lay a horizon without a single tree, just dead dry earth under scorching heat.

---

1. In fact you see nobody at all, only desert.

At the beginning of the 20th century, western adventurers, such as Sven Hadin, Aurel Stein and others who were searching out the ruins and remains of the Silk Road, wrote that they were near death in this place. The most terrifying of the threats was the lack of water and the sudden assault of sandstorms that would unexpectedly appear out of nowhere.

In Stein's description he tells us that midday becomes dark as night, horses whinny, and their manes stream out like the hair of a mad woman. A whole caravan will disappear in the dust of the storm.[2] This kind of storm is a blinding tempest of sand and dust spiraling up 10,000 feet or so; from this tall column the yellow dust will fall on everything below like a heavy smog that settles on everything. (The "sand" is so fine it floats in the air for a long time.)

Confirming the old tales, the fine yellow sand is still stirred up by ferocious winds that carry it to pour down on regions farther to the east. Once while in Beijing I also experienced it as it covered everything there. Sometimes it has even crossed ocean waters to Japan. If we push back through thousands of years we find a period when this dust covered the whole of North China. The famous 4000-year-old Yanshao ruins of the Yellow River (Huang He) Civilization are buried here dozens of meters underground thanks to the yellow soil that poured down on them.

Some time back I was thinking to myself, "Once you hear of a yellow-sand dust storm, don't you want to see it?" In fact, the opportunity really did arise. On entering the Taklimakan Desert, my wife suddenly exclaimed, "Just look at those clouds out there!" Indeed, as we gazed out our car windows, there appeared, as though they had stabbed their way through the surrounding white clouds, strange huge yellow columns of cumulus-nimbus clouds mutely rising before us. Could this really be happening to us?!?

Just as the mushroom cloud of the atomic bomb spread quickly over its area, these clouds, even as we watched, spread out overhead, enveloping everything. People started to run away. They hastily prodded their domestic animals on. Store shutters slammed down. Soon, while all this was happening, the surroundings went dark as night. Then suddenly violent winds attacked from the side. Except for a car moving slowly with its headlights on, nothing could be seen. Surely this furious storm was going to last an hour at most. But again the surrounding area became bright, and when we looked up the blue sky had come back. The wind, however, continued to blow with such force it could push a person who leaned into it erect.

"Oh, the sky's so black!" Something beyond fear affected me. One may wonder whether such a sky might not be the origin of the God of Heaven. Wasn't it on this same way north that an equation was formulated? It is *Kara* = the heavens = blackness = dark mysteries = the Source – and other manifestations of the God

---

2. Quoting *Letters from the Silk Roads*, 40.

of Heaven. You see, then, why it is said that the God of Heaven was born on this northern Silk Road route.

The yellow-sands phenomenon cannot be forecast. Generally many storms hit in the spring at the first of April, but what I saw was in the summertime. The most sophisticated "forecasts" can't indicate any specific place for storms in such a vast desert. I understand that in America even the best-trained weather forecasters cannot pinpoint tornadoes precisely as to time or place.

I wonder whether important aspects of natural phenomena are not replicated in the social realm. At a meeting in which UNESCO was involved, held sometime in the 1980s, I spoke the following words to the gathering: "Today in the world economy Japan seems to be the eye of an economic typhoon toward which high 'winds' blow; this economy attracts the world's money in increasing amounts. The problem is that typhoons *move*." Three years later the bubble burst. And recently (in 1997), from Southeast Asia to Japan an economic crisis has occurred – doesn't it resemble the Yellow Sand crisis? Recently an economist has described the sudden devastating shock to a nation's economy as being similar to a dark cloud turning suddenly into a squall.

In fact, until the summer of 1997 not a single soul predicted the collapse of the East Asian bubble. The collapse certainly attacked the region like a yellow sandstorm.

What we know is that when this kind of storm occurs, there must be an excess of hot, roiling atmosphere at ground level, reminding one of the Southeast Asian economic situation for the last several decades . . . . We might characterize such a situation as *dissatisfaction* with plenty, or a "fullness" that is really never full, or wants that are ever-expanding after basic needs are met. The French Revolution was a time that was so "hot" it created a flash-point that spread like a raging prairie fire.

Near Turfan, in the funeral chamber of Astana, we see a picture of an interesting utensil drawn on the wall. Because of the way it is hung, the glass will dump its contents when full of water. That vividly transmits to us the ancient wisdom of an economics of moderation rather than greed!

Bridge 30

Hattori informs me that Chikuro Hiroike loved this metaphor. Dr. Hiroike was a profound scholar of ethics and religion, and the founder the Institute of "Moralogy" with which Professor Hattori has been actively affiliated for many years. Hiroike has expounded upon such principles as justice and benevolence in inspiring ways.

The utensil he loved is named *Yu Za no Ki*, which I loosely interpret to mean "a self-regulating container that satisfies rather than bloats the drinker." As Dr. Hattori more accurately and specifically explains, "If you fill the vase with water it dumps it; if you fill it by no more than 80% the utensil remains upright."

The drama of the yellow sand storms of Taklimakan, referred to in our subtitle and described as an "encounter" in and of itself, must not distract us from the main topic and title of this chapter, "Black Sky," an idea as Hattori states, "born on the steppe route." The word "black" in this context has many unusual connotations for Western readers, but the main importance for Hattori relates to its part in the cosmological religious and economic values assigned to the four compass directions by Silk Road travelers on land and sea. Travelers went seeking artistic and religious items esteemed as being uniquely precious. Pilgrims were willing to pass through hell risking even death to find such treasures and to bring them home.

Our reflection on the meaning of the storm that Eiji Hattori and his wife encountered emphasizes the extreme lack of certainty in predicting either human or natural catastrophes. Even more importantly, we are seeking to call attention to conditions that bring forth phenomena such as the French Revolution, the change of Chinese dynasties, or, in our times, economic collapse, the fall of Western hegemony or various forms of totalitarianism. These preconditions for catastrophe, while not a basis for precise predictions, may constitute a *moral* warning signaling great trouble ahead for any person or any state that persists too rigidly on a certain path. The path of economic greed or collective revenge should not need the warning, "Do not enter." Our examples are wake-up calls to act wisely on what we already know.

31

The Mountain Sees Rihaku[1]
Images That Move the Mind Toward Quantum Theory

The whole is reflected in each part, and each part, in the whole. That's quantum theory's strange view of existence. It is reminiscent of the ancients' intuition that the *soul* or essence that defines each individual entity somehow corresponds to, and is bound up with, the life of the whole universe.

Recently the 101-year-old Ms. Shizue Katō disclosed her "soul" as one born to be a social activist. In a life coterminous with the full sweep of the 20th century, she helped women improve their status.

I met her 35 years ago when she participated in the meeting of the Inter-Parliamentary Union as an upper house member. Her fluent English was surely a factor in my appreciation of her cosmopolitanism. Her whole being and behavior suited her for the admirable role she has played on the world stage; I have most pleasant memories from our times together in Dakar, Dublin, and Majorca.

I have also encountered her many times in Tokyo. Once, in an almost hour-long chat by telephone on world affairs I listened to her severe criticisms of Japanese society and politics. When I asked her where her seemingly eternal youthfulness comes from, she answered, "About ten times every day I am deeply moved by something or someone."

---

1. Japanese pronunciation of 李白, the name of the famous Chinese poet Li Bai, known as Li Bo or Li Po, "The Poet Immortal."

I'd like to reflect briefly on her passion for whatever is humanly important. The feeling of being touched grows from encounters. A true and pure Encounter with "the other"[2] (a person, a scene of nature, a poem or an event of time) will certainly be accompanied by an emotion that pierces the very soul.[3]

When people have this experience, they can see what a person must see and know what one must know. I recall a vivid instance of this when I saw for the first time a remarkable assemblage of birds and animals often at deadly odds with each other; this viewing occurred in the deep wilds of Tanzania on the shore of a beautiful lake surrounded by the verdure of Tanzania's interior. There, revealed in the brilliant sunlight streaming down on the lake, were numerous species of birds and animals. They were actually living in peace with one another. The purity and innocence of mother earth!

Ah! It's the Garden of Eden!

Here deep encounter and deep emotion were intertwined.

In that decisive moment something was born within me. Then "nature" was no longer just a word in my head, nor was it something I saw with my physical eyes, but now it really and truly sang in my heart. What it brought was not cognitive understanding; it was more akin to boundless love. Also, I would like to identify such an experiential phenomenon as *communication in the deepest sense*.

In a classical poem, Rihaku, a writer of the Tang Dynasty,[4] wrote, "The mountain sees Rihaku." The poet is describing an intuition of "reciprocal vision," which in full form means, "When Rihaku sees the mountain, the mountain sees Rihaku."

At a lecture in Osaka on symbiosis, the French philosopher Augustin Berque, speaking as would an American ecologist, quoted this poem. He distilled its

---

2. "The other" is an important concept in Gabriel Marcel's philosophy of encounter. The concept enunciated here may explain why he was sometimes reluctant to be termed an existentialist, though in other respects he had quite a bit in common with that movement.
3. The "soul" that intrigues Hattori here is one embodied in the physical and embroiled in the circumstances of life. Sometimes personhood in the West evokes an image of detached individuality; an extreme instance of this is the lonely, alienated existentialist. In such distortions of soul, the self may even be imagined as somehow detaching itself from the body or at least the society it despises or from which it wishes to be free. In contrast, the word *shintai*, which I here translate as "the very soul," refers quite literally to either the body or the person. *Body* and *person* are intimately associated. If the body is sometimes a kind of border or boundary of the person – like skin – any significant encounter may in American slang be said to "penetrate even the thickest hide." But, in the vision this book presents, the social and natural worlds are already *in* and *with* each self, without benefit of either isolation or puncture-wound.
4. The Tang was a period (618 to 907) during which the capital of China was still Changan, modern Xian.

essence into the phrase, "thinking like a mountain." He sought to lead us toward a less anthropocentric understanding, moving the center of things from humanity to the cosmos as a whole. Berque's conception is marvelous, but there is a difference between him and the Chinese poet.

When Rihaku views the mountain, he certainly exists as an individual subject. However, Rihaku and the mountain's mutual awareness of each other (each "seeing" the other) actually constitutes what each *comes to be* at the moment they relate. That is what is to be understood from Zen's transmission of the koan[5] that queries us, "What is the sound of one hand clapping?"

Alternatively, we might ask of two hands clapping, "From which hand does sound go out?" This is also a strange question. Perhaps either hand, like the mountain, produces a "sound" other than clapping.

At least we can say of "one hand's clapping" that a "clap" can occur when a one-armed person turns a solitary, private thought or feeling into something public. Perhaps he just unselfconsciously snaps together his two fingers!

What one must notice, from the Zen point of view, is that in true communication where a man and a mountain are, so to speak, *opened up*, they affect the very being of each other.

Isn't such a Zen-like world irrational to the point of absurdity? Certainly classical modern physics since Newton would say so. In fact, however, today's most recent science is coming to confirm the factual truth of this "absurdity." John von Neumann, Henry Stapp and others who have worked on the most advanced frontiers of quantum physics explain the reality of this kind of communication in an astonishing way.

Already, in the first half of the 20th century Niels Bohr, in accordance with the Uncertainty Principle of Werner Heisenberg, had introduced the existence of the "observer" into quantum theory's treatment of the world of the infinitesimal.[6] In other words, he demonstrated scientifically that our consciousness is indispensable

---

5. In his succinct way, Hattori suggests, "Kôan = questions and answers in Zen." On the worldwide web, Wikipedia expands this: "A *kōan* (公案; Japanese: *kōan*, Chinese: *gōng-àn*, Korean: *gong'an*, Vietnamese: *công án*) is a story, dialogue, question, or statement in the history and lore of Chán (Zen) Buddhism, generally containing aspects that are inaccessible to rational understanding, yet may be accessible to intuition."
6. One version of Heisenberg's principle states, "The more precisely position is determined the less precisely momentum is known." In defiance of common sense, our "knowing" of position with accuracy seems to interfere with what can be known of momentum and vice versa. It's as though, seeking to "see" something somehow changes what we are looking at. We were aware of this peril as we studied people, and most of all as we sought by introspection to study ourselves. But somehow mountains and electrons conceived by us as mere objective *things* shouldn't "talk back" this way! The "observed" mountain shouldn't shout back at Rihaku, "I see what you're doing, you're changing me!"

to the very makeup of any phenomenal thing we may "observe." Observers should no longer think of themselves as "spectators." They, too, are in the scene.

Furthermore, in recent years, Stapp continues to refer to Von Neumann's "probability wave" as well as to the concept of *event*. He proved that the freedom, which is the property of God alone in the mechanistic universe of classical physics, can now be accorded also to human beings.

In the midst of this discussion Stapp explains the importance of *faith*. What he says is that when a human being exercises faith by choosing one possible action among several, that choice suddenly changes the probability wave so that it becomes concentrated in the decision.[7] This change is called a "quantum jump." It suggests that people need to realize more than ever that they are masters of their destiny, not in spite of nature, but because freedom is entirely natural.

In contrast to physics as taught in the schools, top-of-the-line physics on the frontiers of knowledge is elucidating reality in terms of the inseparability of subject and object. It goes without saying that Einstein's work in relativity laid the groundwork for this discovery.

Quantum theory's ontology holds that all subatomic particles in the universe communicate in a way that transcends time and space, and that each such tiny entity is reflected in the whole at the same time that the whole is reflected in each such particle. Uncannily, this theory corresponds to the insight of some of our ancestors who declared that the individual soul is linked directly to the great life of the universe, involving communication with the whole. This insight was part of the unexpected discovery of tradition by science, as expressed by the Venice Declaration of 1986.[8]

Our movement of soul consists of direct participation in the formation of the universe. In this theory, emotion is a manifestation of life at any given moment . . . . Such moments only arrive in a mind open for what we are calling Deep Encounters.

Bridge 31

A catalyst for this essay was the Chinese poem by Li Bai alias Rihaku (701-762). In it the poet is reflecting on an experience he had while sitting alone on a mountain. We here append the original Chinese and our English paraphrase.

---

7. Hattori has pointed out that this kind of thinking joins Minakata's in terms of an "encounter point." I think that is also called a gathering point. For more on Minakata see our next chapter, Encounter 32.
8. A declaration from a UNESCO-convened seminar in which we find the words: "This... enriching exchange between science and the different traditions of the world opens the door to a new vision of humanity, and even to a new rationalism, which could lead to a new metaphysical perspective."

獨座敬亭山

衆鳥高飛盡
孤雲獨去閑[9]
相看兩不厭
唯有敬亭山

Facing the Mountain Alone

A multitude of birds are wearied from flying high
near a bow-shaped cloud, while I pass my leisure alone.
The mountain and I are never bored – we
just exist and look at each other[10]

It is appropriate to end this with a "www summary" of Quantum Physics that begins with a fact little appreciated by most lay readers in physics. "We are all familiar with the motion of particles from our every-day experience with solid objects. Like balls on a billiards table, when two particles run into each other, they bounce apart. In contrast, when two waves meet, they pass right through each other!" I am quoting from an article on the web entitled "Quantum Waves." Though somewhat technical, the article can be heartily recommended as a summary of Quantum Physics and the controversies it has raised among scientists and philosophers. The "moving-picture" graphic illustrates wave theory in a stunning way! (Access at www.physics.uiowa.edu)

---

9. This 閑 is the Japanese character. I do not have the old Chinese character in my character set, but the meaning is the same.
10. The crucial word here, as Hattori has already indicated, is 相看. It seems not to be a discrete word in Japanese but a compound of *ai* + *mi* = mutual + seeing (or watching) One dictionary relates the compound to the original Chinese word in such a way as to include in its meaning *looking after* or *caring for*. This nuance would support Hattori's cosmic-human interpretation of both quantum theory and the poem.

32

Night Thoughts Occasioned by a Falling Star
Causality (因, IN) and Supercausality (縁, EN)

A night of falling stars.... Fine golden sand scattered about on heaven's jet-black canopy....The Milky Way smoldering there dimly.... Suddenly what I saw made me feel something familiar, very close to my core.... Bottomless mystery .... Profound silence.... The incomprehensible then appeared to my mind as infinitely tender.

"*This eternal silence of infinite space makes me tremble in fear.*" These words of Pascal, which had for long haunted me, now, in one nocturnal flash, began to leave me in silence. My usual confidence in Pascal's *Pensées* (the collection of literary fragments from which this thought is drawn) had relied too much on 17th century "reasonings" regarding evil. These developments signaled the beginning of the Modern Age. Infinite space engendered a vision of space without God. Much as I admire Pascal, his trembling and the whisperings of anxiety in my soul turned out to be nothing other than the culmination of irrational fears engendered by "Reason."[1]

My experience has shown me how "reason" in its modern form engages in simplification. In fact, the path of modern science tends to reduce the complex universe too exclusively into its elements.

The 19th century was devoted to the Law of Causality. "Cause" and "effect" were the two correlated terms that were thought to explain everything. According

---

1. In correspondence, Hattori adds, "In the beginning of the Modern Age, Reason becomes the dominant faculty. Humans lose the holistic view of Reality."

to one understanding of "cause," it is what makes things happen. As the British writer Lesslie Newbigin puts it, "Things are to be explained in terms of their causes . . . All causes are adequate to the effects they produce."[2] Now suppose we accept this definition of "cause." Even so, the proposition about adequacy, or similarity between cause and effect, is *not* congruent with actual phenomena. Why isn't it?

An important presupposition of Buddhist tradition is that this world is permeated by *en* (a Japanese word for connection, providence, chance, karma, webbed threads – or some combination of these). The person who opened my eyes to this was Ms. Kazuko Tsurumi. Her thought, as reflected here, is based on the research of Minakata Kumagusu (1867-1941).[3]

The time was 1992. I well remember the day when Ms. Tsurumi and I entered the primeval forest along the Amazon River. "Wonderful! Great! See what is growing from the trunk of the cacao tree!"[4] She was very animated. At an international conference in Balem, Brazil, this very cosmopolitan person manifested her natural behavior with her usual spontaneity. At the conference she was introduced to the world as an ecological pioneer; Minakata was identified as a Japanese genius who has lived in relative obscurity while laboring on the frontiers of knowledge.

Minakata Kumugusu pays special attention to two Buddhist concepts, which he refers to as "causality" and "*en*":

> In today's science we understand causality, but we do not understand *en*. *En* is born of a congestion of causes, so my task is to seek the Causality of Causalities in their ensemble.[5]

---

2. I have here inserted Lesslie Newbigin's statement from his *The Gospel in a Pluralist Society* (SPCK, 1989, p. 36). Readers of philosophical English may find the insertion clarifies somewhat what Hattori is explaining here. The fundamental concern of both writers is that whichever way we interpret the analytic, mechanistic understanding of causality, modern scientism renders purpose and value meaningless and God optional except in a purely deterministic sense. Even the latter was unacceptable for the astronomer-mathematician Laplace who opined, "God is an unnecessary hypothesis."
3. As a biologist, Minakata is probably most widely recognized for his explorations into the world of molds, but he was a polymath who is just coming into our consciousness in the West.
4. Ms. Tsurumi undoubtedly was remarking on the fruit, which comes out straight from the trunk, not from a branch as one would expect.
5. Gordon Mercer is a scholarly and sensitive friend of mine. He suggests that synchronicity is the term evoked by his reading of the present chapter. In connection with the Complexity and Chaos theories, he feels, as the psychiatrist Jung is reported to have felt, that at least some coincidences may not be "mere" coincidences. "Synchronicity" helps Mercer keep this important distinction in mind.

In a letter addressed to Toki Horyu, the high priest of the Shingon sect of Buddhism,[6] Minakata emphasized that what he was saying was not a denial of causality but an affirmation of the fact that a series of causes will intertwine with other such series to birth a complexity of interactions. From this dynamic intertwining arises *mutual influence*. (In formal discussions of Buddhist philosophy *dependent co-origination* is the term usually applied to this phenomenon.)

According to this kind of interaction, phenomena that on first glance scatter into disorder and chaos may in certain times and places *generate mutual attraction* to produce convergence on a point, a "gathering point" as Minakata terms it. His view of things was anticipating what is now designated as Complexity Theory.

There's a wonderfully strange figure drawn by Minakata; it depicts an intersection of both points and lines. Dr. Hajime Nakamura, whom Ms. Tsurumi asked to look at the figure, promptly exclaimed, "Oh, it's the Minakata Mandala, isn't it?" Eventually the designation Minakata Mandala became the standard name for this unique drawing,[7] but now it has gained attention as something showing us a scientific model of a new future that goes beyond what we have heretofore thought of as "modern science." Moreover, this is not some kind of daydream but something based on detailed scientific observations and inferences.

My thoughts fly from the primeval mountain forests of Nachi[8] as described by Minakata, and far beyond into the depths of the sky and the Infinite Universe.

Now we have marvelous images of breathtaking beauty transmitted from the Hubble satellite space telescope and from Subaru. Subaru is the new astronomical telescope established by Japan on the Island of Hawaii for cooperation in study of the Pleiades. In these images I see a close interrelationship with the Minakata Mandala, which antedated astronomical photography by decades. Isn't it just possible that Minakata's smallest world and the Subaru telescope's grandest findings really constitute one cosmos?

The birth of the universe, which is said to have occurred with the Big Bang some fifteen billion years ago, alerts us in a fuller way than ever before to the infinitely expanding dimensions of our cosmos. In its whirling mass, we find

---

6. Kūkai (774-835) is the founder of the Shingon (True Word) sect in Japan. Readers interested in the religious and philosophic antecedents of Kūkai's Japanese version of Esoteric Tantric Buddhism may consult the chapter on him in John C. Plott's *Global History of Philosophy* series, IV, 121-133. Plott classifies him as one of the many exponents of "Monism in Many Moods" during the period 800-900. In many respects, Kūkai's type of Buddhism is a leading example of this-worldly or even world-affirming enlightenment in which nothing and no one high or low outshines another . . . .
7. In the period from 1901 to 1903 while still in his early 30s and corresponding with Toki Horyu, Kumagusu "revealed his concept of the universe" – "Minakata Mandala"! Cited from "The Life's journey of Kumagusu" (Minakata Kumagusu Museum) at minakatakumagusu-kinenkan.jp/english/kumagusu/lifemap, accessed on 4-26-2007.
8. A traditional abode of gods.

numberless stars studding the Milky Way, including black holes sucking up its light. When the rare death of a massive star occurs, the resulting supernova explosion proceeds to create an immense cloud of fine dust particles. They swim around in a dark universe until, on occasion, they begin to attract each other and even assemble themselves. In this way new stars are born. Aren't the images of these events like the single-frames in the evolutionary "movie" of Life?

My life is but an infinitesimal speck among all the tiny star fragments, a bit of dust brought fully alive by means of innumerable encounters with other people and the Great Life or living form called Universe. Just as a star meets and welcomes its death, so I as a single reassembly point also welcome mine.

However, each point is part of the whole cosmos. Such points will shatter and reassemble as they have shattered and reassembled before. The beauty of this process floats tranquilly along on the ever-flowing river of time. . . .

As for that night of falling stars, I have "breathed" many breaths of encounter since then.

Bridge 32

A reverent person may see in the extreme contractions, explosive dispersals, and reassemblies of bits of cosmic dust an intimation of "God's Divine Body," as if it were inhaling and exhaling. At any rate Hattori does not simply "see" or "feel" or "think." He breathes the sweet aroma of Universe. This is not pantheism, it is panentheism (Cosmos *in* God, not God = Cosmos). Actually our return to the "simple" may involve the acceptance of falling apart (death and dying) before a new reordering and re-creation can take place.

When Hattori writes of falling stars, that is reminiscent of the old Afro-American spiritual, "My Lord, what a morning; oh, my Lord, what a morning, when the stars begin to fall!"[9] New Testament visioning appears to emphasize one climactic Kingdom-Coming, while *assembly, dissolution and reassembly* characterize Hattori's summation. No matter whether chaos and evil are singularly or serially reversed, their *defeat* is the decisive point in common.

Lest we conclude that this rather impersonal and abstract discussion discloses the whole tone of Hattori's philosophy of religion, we may need to recall Encounter 10 where, in reference to Paul's affirmation of "Christ in me," Hattori comments, "People who say things like this have in common an intuitive feeling that whatever acts as the foundation of the universe is not a cold, stationary point but a living love that is Life itself."

---

9. Based on one vision of the end of the world – its destruction preparatory for a new creation *on earth* as described in Revelation 6:12-13. Another creative aspect of such destruction is brought out by Paul in 1 Corinthians 15:51-58.

Among the many fields of Minakata's expertise beyond modern biological science, the most outstanding is his creative philosophizing and his intimate awareness of traditional Japanese culture. His approximately forty volumes of writings are still being archived, their continuing timeliness increasingly appreciated.

Part IV
The Ultimate Glow
Pulling It All Together

A Modern Burning Bush

Previous chapters have nominated nature as one important model for freeing humanity from problems requiring a mixture of complex and simple solutions. What I am looking at is neither exactly burning nor exactly a bush, but it is a miracle of nature. A recent issue of *National Geographic* ("Swarm Theory," July 2007) shows a large bushy tree aflame with the glow of fireflies, thousands of fireflies.

They probably do not know why they are there or how they happened to get there, but the gathering is due to random individual actions that operate within a certain short list of simple rules of benefit to the whole species.

The caption to this stunning picture causes me to wonder if human bottom-up behavior, given the right rules, might improve the future for our species and its nurturing environment. In the case of the firefly, each individual adjusts its firing to the flashes of the others in ways robotic experiments can replicate. The human benefits? "Such self-organized behavior resembles the synchronized firing of heart muscle cells or the rhythmic applause of a crowd – but seems more mysterious." (p.144)

Instances of "lower species" whose self-organizing behavior provides or promises solutions for human conundrums are: how to have no leader of a group yet more creative and efficient decision-making, finding the most efficient delivery routes for trucking, managing heavy traffic flow, protecting a group from outside harm, including flushing out terrorists with robots.

Jared Diamond's important book *Collapse: How Societies Choose to Fail or Succeed* contains success stories of societies large and small that have chosen to succeed either by top-down leadership or a bottom-up push that is sometimes self-consciously purposeful and sometimes not. Success can be a mixture of "top-down" and "bottom-up" initiative and cooperation.

One cannot help but ask whether our world might somehow blunder or reason or wonder itself into success in a similar fashion as the birds, the bees, and some cultures. To open up new approaches to these natural or cosmic solutions, approaches that combine the best of current scientific research with the best of the "deep traditions," read on.

33

Japan for the World
Noh Theater as Change-Agent in the 21st Century

I feel like I want to turn our country's head away from the century we've just passed through, a century full of terrible shocks and violent upheavals.

Whatever criticisms may be made of Japan, I believe most of us who inhabit this chain of islands want to recover *wa*, a harmonious spirit in our land, a spirit that still seeks to lodge itself deeply in Japanese hearts. That kind of spirit is even evident in ancient Japanese drama as found in Noh and Kabuki. What deserves special attention in such plays is the absence of a special director of scenes. That function is performed by the single actor occupying the point of focus. He is central because his every breath in or out directs all else on stage. Innumerable invisible threads link actors and musicians. From that center of attention the action naturally flows and develops so what happens on stage is not constituted or controlled by an off-stage eye, as in Western drama.[1]

Who is the leading actor in Noh? To answer in the Western way, it is what the actor called *shite* seems to be.

However, in the Noh, *shite* is mostly one whose story is narrated by a *waki*, the "second" actor.[2] The latter occupies a spot of real life from which he pushes the plot along, unfolding what we might call the tale of an apparition, that of

---

1. Hattori's handwritten note clarifies, "In Western theatre a stage director (not to mention a choreographer . . .) is looking at the stage and giving instructions."
2. The *waki* is a supporting or "side" player. According to one source, "he is the counterpart or foil of the *shite*."

the *shite*. (Almost all Noh stories are stories of apparitions.) The music, too, is in harmony with the *waki's* tale and its telling, and thus constitutes an essential element in Noh.

Midway in the story, the *shite* appears like colored horizontal thread (the woof or weft) in brocade (*nishiki*) and soon fades away. In Western theatre, the leading actor sees, speaks and acts. But in Japanese Noh theatre, the *shite* is called upon to appear and ultimately to vanish.

The make-up or pattern of everything that revolves around the lead is like a great stream of consciousness. In it, the proper Japanese style of living is one in which not a single thread is out of order; this style discloses itself in beauty shrouded in mystery (yūgen, 幽玄[3]). Once, on his day of arrival in Japan, Roland Barth[4] compressed his wonder and admiration into these words, "In Japan there is a vacuum in the center." (This refers not to a moral vacuum, which is another important issue – see Chapter 20 above, for example – but to a tradition in which the individual is not "full of himself or herself.")

It is apparent that the magnetic goal of leadership shaped by the quest for power alone can create doom and havoc right and left. Shouldn't we reconsider our need once more to meditate on the "heart" of *wa* as exemplified in Noh drama?

和
wa

Bridge 33

The authors hope that the character *wa* is, in its deepest meaning, a foreshadowing of Japan's contribution to a world we all like to envision as guided by more beautiful, humane, quiet, and peaceful ways than any of us consistently experience in our daily grind. In this respect the Japanese word 和 and the Hebrew word shalom deserve careful comparison and reflection. This chapter is the conclusion of the original Japanese book and perhaps our most compressed expression of the Japanese cultural heritage.

Next, we turn to a somewhat more Western-style of exposition. We hope there to paint a world that is turning itself not toward another chapter of violence and or escapist indifference but toward an energy-filled quietude – *wa* and *shalom* come to earth.

---

3. One dictionary definition of the important term *yūgen* is "subtle profundity."
4. I believe this to be the American educator. "Roland S. Barth is a former public school teacher and principal. He was founding director of the Principals' Center at Harvard University and the author of several books . . . ." Credit: The Rhode Island Foundation.

A Japanese complement to wa is *yūgen*, which Arthur Waley, the early 20th century expositor of Zeami (Seami), explains with liberal use of Zeami's own words:

> It means "what lies beneath the surface; the subtle, as opposed to the obvious; the hint, as opposed to the statement. It is applied to the natural grace of a boy's movements; to the gentle restraint of a nobleman's speech and bearing. "When notes fall sweetly and flutter delicately to the ear," that is the *yūgen* of music. The symbol of *yūgen* is "a white bird with flower in its beak." "To watch the sun sink behind a flower-clad hill, to wander on and on in a huge forest with no thought of return, to stand upon the shore and gaze after a boat that goes hid by far-off islands, to ponder on the journey of wild-geese seen and lost among the clouds" – such are the gates to *yūgen*.[5]

Whether this soft and subtle background can survive and perhaps enhance direct and directive prescriptions for our day is an issue that will challenge both authors and readers in the rest of Part IV.

As we turn to the problems of UNESCO, the problematic leadership of the USA, and the holistic understanding of each and all of the elements in our chaotic, yet self-ordering cosmos, the question of the day becomes, "What constructive perspective, program of action, or sustaining faith emerges from all this?"

---

5. Arthur Waley, *The Nō Plays of Japan* (New York: Grove Press, 1957), 21-22.

34

UNESCO for the World
Controversy and Movement
From Both Sides of the Hattori/Gray Bridge

As alluded to in chapter 12, critics of UNESCO's financial soundness pointed out that UNICEF, the United Nations children's fund, raised its much larger budget with relative ease and entirely from voluntary contributions, while UNESCO was experiencing difficulties gaining approval for UN mandated support. A *Reuter's* report (March 9, 2000) contains the comment, "But nobody wants to give to an organization whose mission is unclear and whose headquarters are top-heavy with bureaucrats." Perhaps more germane to UNESCO's funding difficulties is the fact that it is harder to attract significant contributions on behalf of education, science, and culture than on behalf of children. The reason is that too few potential supporters of UNESCO see children's needs as intersecting significantly with the words in UNESCO'S name and commission: United Nations Educational, Scientific, and Cultural Organization.

In the English edition of the well-regarded Japanese daily, *The Asahi Shimbun* (Saturday-Sunday, November 30-December 1, 2002), Hattori gave careful analysis of how UNESCO's history was intertwined with U.S. leadership in the world at the time. He gave the positives and the negatives, first summarizing global developments at the time:

Shocking revelations about abductions of Japanese nationals by the Democratic People's Republic of Korea (North Korea), U.S. threat to attack Iraq and escalated antagonism between Israel and the Palestinians have dominated the news in recent months.

Amid such striking developments, however, was an incident that drew little media attention. It is the return of the United States to the United Nations Educational, Scientific and Cultural Organization (UNESCO).

The announcement came at the end of a long campaign by UNESCO Director General Koichiro Matsuura, the first Japanese to head the agency, to encourage the United States to come back into the fold. This is no doubt good news, and I welcome it.

At the same time, however, I do not feel completely comfortable with the change of heart. Washington has yet to dispel suspicion its return is aimed at dodging international criticism of U.S. unilateralism. Immediately after announcing its reconciliation with UNESCO, the White House began to publicize the policy program, the Bush doctrine, with a strong tint of unilateralism....

After a series of reforms, including budgetary allocations to key projects, enhanced transparency in personnel management and operational streamlining, UNESCO cut in half the number of department chiefs and higher posts.

In fact, the three problems[1] that estranged the United States in the 1980s had disappeared during the presidency of Bill Clinton, who pushed a policy of international cooperation. Clinton tried to win Congressional approval for the $60 million (about 7.2 billion yen) needed to rejoin the organization, but the bid was turned down by the Republican-controlled Senate.

Unlike his internationalist predecessor, Bush and his Republican administration have turned to a policy of unilateralism, pursuing U.S. interests above all others. Given the circumstances, it is natural to assume that the United States returned to UNESCO for one reason, namely the Sept. 11, 2001, terrorist attacks....

Washington must do away with the idea of U.S.-centric globalization and the supremacist presumption that "American justice is global justice."

It must make an effort to understand cultural diversity and traditional values sought by people of different ethic backgrounds. Only when the United States acquires the humility to learn from others can it consider itself a true friend of international society.

* * *

Before my retirement from Southwestern College where I have taught for 40 years (and continue to work in academic endeavors such as this book), we on the faculty crafted a vision statement still in effect today. Its fourth and final call describes the kind of learning community the college aspires to be globally. It is one that nurtures "leadership through service in a world without boundaries."

---

1. Background history on the three problems is found in Chapter 12 above.

Students and patrons of the college are hearing the call.

In the summer of 2007 Amanda Salzman, a Southwestern College sophomore and news intern for the *Winfield Daily Courier* shared her impressions (for the issue of August 18, 2007) of a conference in Washington, D.C. The conference was sponsored by the Atlantic Council and Americans for Informed Democracy, and its keynote speaker was Gillian Sorenson, senior advisor and national advocate at the United Nations Foundation and the former Assistant Secretary General of the United Nations.

When student Salzman boarded her plane home, exhausted but inspired, she recalled Sorenson's "optimism [as] contagious, her message of change, encouraging: America is good, but it can be better."

Sorenson's comments as an American strikingly parallel what Hattori advocates as a Japanese supporter of the UN and UNESCO. Sorenson's words:

> "After 12 years of unpaid United Nations dues and dismissals of the organization as 'incompetent and lazy,' the U.S. must rejoin the international community by rejoining the U.N." She insists that the U.S. develop a foreign policy with "coherence," one that "reflects the morals of the country...."
>
> "We need to let the world know we can cooperate, that we're not the big bully."

In the next chapter I hope to engage more deeply with the disturbing issues raised by Hattori and Sorenson.

35

USA for the World
Humility and Arrogance

Editor's Introduction. This chapter contains a further severe critique of American foreign policy from Hattori's point of view. As co-author and editor, and strictly for the benefit of dialogue, I am proposing, as the only American in sight, to introduce the principal speaker and, on behalf of my fellow-citizens, to sit tight with focused attention for a minute or so. Only after this painful but necessary discipline will I start any kind of rebuttal from my hot seat. I hope here to model for fellow-Americans a way of dealing productively with criticisms such as leveled by Sorenson and Hattori in the previous chapter. The hot seat must not be allowed to affect a cool head. To take the stance I am recommending is not to surrender to anything untrue or unfair. Mild mannered people must not confuse the amount of heat necessary to warm the house or cook a tasty meal with an out-of-control fire that burns the whole place down. (Since this whole chapter is dialogical, there will be no isolated Bridge. In its entirety the chapter will function as a bridge between the authors and readers, as well as between the two authors themselves.)

In an essay entitled, *Distorsion civilizationelle et terroisme – Couper la chaine de la haine*,[1] Hattori, writing in French, expresses what we have here presented in English. Let readers (particularly American readers) pay close heed to the case he builds for "cutting the shackles of hate."

---

1. Essay in the UNESCO Publication entitled, *Eiji Hattori: Selection of Essays in French and English* from the Symposium "Cultural Diversity and Transversal Values," UNESCO, 2005.

Of course terrorism must be punished severely... but *90%*, the percentage of those supporting the U.S. president, who after 9-11 immediately declared vengeance, presents a terrifying tableau of a people in fury who for a moment were losing control.

"Wanted, dead or alive.

"You are with us or you are against us."

These words are perfect for a film of the Wild West genre. They are not words of reason. They are words of wrath. And nothing is further from the Christian spirit than words of "vengeance."

Editor's Comment

"Not reason"? *"Not Christian spirit"*? This is strong language, indeed.

For me as Hattori's editor, co-author, and friend, these words sting every time I read them, but then I remember the quotation from Sorenson in the preceding chapter in which she argues for an American foreign policy that "reflects the morals of the country."

In the very week when I was working on this chapter, a furious and unbalanced gunman shot and killed five or six Amish children in their American school. Some of the older children offered to substitute their lives for those younger if the gunman would at least spare the little ones. He did not. Nevertheless, the Amish banded together in prayer for the killer (who also killed himself) and his family. This set of actions I counterpose to the vengeance Hattori complains of in the Bush response to 9-11. Amish behavior in this and many other instances is exemplary of Americans at their best. However, I realize that such behavior cannot directly be translated into foreign policy. Can less complicated institutions incorporate this kind of approach in their policies?

There is much evidence that they can. For example, the church in which I am an active participant has a group of prisoners and parolees in services every Sunday. I am a member of this church's Prison Ministry Team. We are a link between the community to which many of these men will someday be returned and the state corrections authorities who are running out of space in which to have them re-incarcerated. Our purpose is not to further punish these individuals but to help them redirect their lives. We do not minimize the harm they have done themselves and their society; neither do we seek revenge for it, even when they relapse.

More pertinent still to 9-11 is a news release the headline of which sings of cooperation, reason, and interfaith reverence for human life and need.

United Methodists, Muslims partner to ease suffering

The article's leading paragraph is eloquent in its implications:

Religious leaders, diplomats, British government ministers and members of Parliament are praising the new partnership between United Methodist and Muslim relief agencies, [a partnership] that "confounds stereotypes and is both *bold* and *significant*."[2]

However, Hattori is firmly convinced that the problem is not primarily between religions but ethnic groups, so let's continue to hear him out.

Vengeance calls forth vengeance. Hatred creates hatred.

The war of vengeance was launched with terrifying fire power against a country of extreme poverty which had already exhausted its provisions due to three years of drought and had entered a severe winter. More than two million refugees crossed the mountains with nothing except their clothing. But the most miserable would be too poor even to become refugees. Five million innocent persons are already on the verge of starvation. The majority of these are women and children.

When Mr. Bush blocked the frontiers and cried, "We will cut off supplies to the Taliban," didn't the image of these persons, victims of a war that had already continued for twenty years, ever cross his mind? And the whole world that had shed tears for the three thousand irreplaceable lives lost in the World Trade Center did nothing for two months but look on as more than a hundred times that number of lives were in imminent danger of being lost. When events took that course, were these victims overlooked because they were mere heathens? Or was it because they were poor?

In the same UNESCO collection of essays and speeches we find the lecture-essay, "The Significance of Islam in the Dialogue among Civilizations." In it Hattori takes issue with the central idea of Samuel P. Huntington's celebrated essay, "The Clash of Civilizations." That essay predicted a global clash of "Christian" and "Islamic" civilizations, but Hattori asserts:

Civilizations do not clash. It is ignorance that clashes.

It is ignorance of civilizations. Regrettably such ignorance is now conspicuous among those in power, who are leading the world....

Since Arabs who had converted to Islam came from Morocco to the southern tip of Spain at the beginning of the 8th century, Muslims, Jews, and Christians lived together in peace for as long as five centuries, and their cultural marriage gave birth to brilliant works of art and architecture. They also rediscovered natural science and the philosophy of ancient Greece, which they translated into Arabic and Latin....

Hattori contends that for too long history books have contained a "warp."

---

2. Source: http://www.umc.org/site/apps/nlnet/content3.aspx?c=lwL4KnN1LtH&b=2072519&ct=4029451. Accessed on 2-26-08. Later developments on this front continue to inspire hope for better days ahead.

The illusion that Western civilization is the one and only civilization has been shared not only by people of Europe and the United States, but also by non-Westerners until quite recently. Why? It is because textbooks written by colonial powers during the colonial period spread around the world.

People in the Arab world harbor deep resentment that their own culture, their human dignity, has thus been ignored. . . .

At this point I would simply interrupt to point out that it is a related but different issue whether a given culture criticized from the outside has in fact degenerated from its Golden Days. The civilization in moral collapse might be Western Christian or Muslim Middle Eastern. In either case, the tangled pattern of causation that brought things to this low point would take long and tedious research to unwind. But surely we can agree that it is never a good practice to treat another whole *people* with condescension or contempt.

Let us listen to the rest of Hattori's argument.

Of the resentment I was speaking of, we should realize that such resentment, or what Mahdi Elmandjra (of Morocco) calls "humiliation," is the very hotbed of terrorism. The cause of terrorism is not poverty, though people often oversimplify it as such. The root cause of terrorism is unfairness, i.e. injustice.

What we are required to do now is to become truly civilized. A civilized person is one who knows himself and tries to learn from others; one who knows and respects the difference of cultures; and one who seeks the transversal[3] values of humanity found in all these cultures.

An American philosopher wraps up the values of which Hattori speaks in a single phrase, *bare reverence*.[4] Bare reverence underlies and overarches cultural and even "religious" differences and conflicts. Truly *deep* encounters with each other's humanity will inspire the thoughtfully reverent to find alternatives to the chaotic and injurious aspects of "9-11" and its aftermath. Our best imaginations can invent untried solutions and prompt us to test them in action. We hope our book is a stimulus to move in this direction, but I must not evade my American responsibility to answer some of Hattori's severest strictures on our country.

Eiji and readers, it may help to remember our country's relatively short memory concerning former "enemies." Our own civil war may have produced our longest lasting and most internally restrictive feeling of alienation. But both the Marshall plan in Europe and the continuing global activities of the Peace Corps[5] show American official policy at its best. Unfortunately, some of our

---

3. Yes, "transversal" is a word, though new to me. In math and generally, it means *intersecting*.
4. See Paul Woodruff's *Reverence: Renewing a Forgotten Virtue* (Oxford University Press, 2001), particularly the opening pages of Chapter Five, "Ancient Greece: the way of being human," the story of Croesus, Solon and Cyrus, 81-85.
5. Consult "Cross-Cultural Solutions" on the internet for details or simply Google "Peace Corps" for the years of interest.

country's recent bellicose reactions to terrorism may cast an opaque shadow over such history and even over continuing benevolent efforts carried on by volunteers worldwide.

To respond more directly to Hattori's challenging analysis I turn to the U.S. Election Year of 2008. In length and quality it was an excruciating time, even for the most conscientious and well-informed American voters. For that very reason it gives us a suitable case study in the effort to understand and perhaps rectify our admittedly flawed relationship with other countries, cultures, and peoples.

The extreme rhetoric about Iraq as I sit writing in my American kitchen is confusing, irrelevant, and sometimes downright silly:

"Stay the course no matter what the cost!"

"NO! Withdraw all troops immediately, or by such and such a date."

"You lied about what I did or said on such and such a date!"

(The rhetoric noticeably improved after Election Day, but for how long?) There is no arithmetically clear way to find the Golden Mean in the midst of all the nonsense, but some of the most level-headed military and civilian leaders agree that political and restorative efforts are more important in the long run than anything of a military nature. Let me qualify that. If inter-ethnic or interreligious violence prevents rebuilding the infrastructure, and with it the hopes of Iraqi people "great and small," then some form of police-restraining will be necessary, but how about making it as multilateral internally and externally as possible? There is evidence off and on of modest gains in cease-fires and in the orderliness to shield survivors from further "collateral damage."[6]

In our concluding chapter's summing up, we shall elaborate on some major sources of hope in connection with principal issues discussed in this book. We Americans should thank Hattori for forcing us to suspend our national pride long enough to look these issues more "straight in the eye." With better information and sharper vision, we may yet renew the possibility for some altruistic luster to adhere to whatever globally beneficial activities we engage in.

An obvious piece of advice for other Americans as confused and anxious as I am is to keep informed. Read, read, and read some more! Learn to think critically and creatively. Turn off the noisy radio, the redundant TV, the demanding internet, and other distractions long enough to read *one* illuminating book such as *The Shia Revival: How Conflicts within Islam Will Shape the Future* by Vali Nasr (W.W. Norton & Co., 2006-07). Nasr writes knowledgeably about the issue of which Muslim leaders seem to show the most potential for dealing with the tragic divisions within Islam.

---

6. Translation: killing, maiming, bereaving, rendering homeless, embittering and further impoverishing persons whose only wrong was being at the wrong place at the wrong time, or even being asleep in their own homes.

36

A Holistic Philosophy for Each and All
Towards Transcultural Dialogue[1]

The preceding chapters have granted us many glimpses into Eiji Hattori's life and thought as he encounters specific events, issues, peoples, cultures, and individuals. The present chapter melds all these glimpses into one philosophical and cultural synthesis of his philosophy. This essay also reveals UNESCO'S raison d'être as well as Hattori's significant role in its programs. – Editor

"What would a community of nations amount to without a community of minds?" was the question posed by Paul Valéry at the dawn of the new era following the Second World War.

These words of the poet of the Midi[2] were quoted by François Mitterrand in his address to the Member States at the 1993 session of the General Conference of UNESCO. The French President went on to say: "Indeed, a great prospect, ladies and gentlemen: a place where the idea of a right to culture would take shape,

---

1. This essay, translated by an anonymous but expert scholar, provides the philosophical basis for future "deep encounters." Adapted from the English-language essay, "Toward a transcultural dialogue: the role of UNESCO in the development of transdisciplinarity" and published in *Reitaku Journal of Interdisciplinary Studies* Vol. 5. No. 2, September, 1997. Presented for the UNESCO Symposium "Cultural Diversity and Transversal Values," 2005.
2. Midi is a cultural region in the south of France where Paul Valéry's birthplace, Sète, is located.

together with international projects for exchanges and co-operation between the great civilizations." This led him to the conclusion that "your real objective is surely to re-establish links with the community of minds."

This remark becomes increasingly relevant to a time when, as the second millennium draws to a close, we are witnessing a phenomenon that might be termed the "desertification of the mind," which goes hand in hand with our agonizing awareness of the ever more glaringly apparent "desertification of the planet."

The linear conception of time, from which the notion of progress stems, must surely have been largely responsible for creating this situation, which imperils not just nature but our species as a whole.

The roots of the problem are to be found in the fundamental principles of material civilization – a principle based on the belief in the omnipotence of science and technology. This notion dates back to the seventeenth century, a period in which the natural sciences – then regarded as the antithesis of theology – made their first advances, opening up new and promising prospects for the well-being of humankind. This belief reached its peak in the nineteenth century with its doctrine of "scientism."

But, one might ask, was not this very principle of material civilization itself grounded in premises that had never been challenged: namely (1) that nature is inexhaustible, and (2) that *Homo sapiens* is outside nature and is entitled to conquer and master it?

Since Descartes, the philosophical claim that mind and body were two separate entities was taken for granted and its truth seemed to have been borne out by the success of Newtonian science and its *subject-object dualism*, originating in ancient Greece and revived during the Renaissance. This line of thinking proved to be conducive to science, which offers humanity the "Good Life" in place of the "Gospel" (Good News). *Cogito*, or rather *Dubito*, affirms the existence of self – *ego sum* (I am) – but ignores the being (*Esse*) of others. From the time of Descartes onwards, a different "West" emerged which sought to discard the spiritual tradition that had once informed the whole Continent. The notion of family was gradually set aside to make room for the *universal*. Those who had been baptized in reason rather than in the Holy Ghost believed themselves to be on the only road leading to truth and reality. Yet in this civilization that was thought to be new, the individual ("*I*") began to feel increasingly lonely. After the era of the great philosophical systems, and even at a time of anti-philosophical thinking or of existentialism, the "I" was desperately lonely when confronted with God (*Kierkegaard*) or with nothingness (*Sartre*) – "Hell is other people" – until structuralism, with the support of linguistic and cultural anthropology, finally dethroned the "I". It has to be acknowledged that Sartre's despair, based on a fundamental solipsism, had been insidiously nurtured by Descartes.[3] It is no accident that both of them were planning a final work on ethics – works that never saw the light of day.

The will to selfhood, which is lonely by definition, entails the will to power, as described by Nietzsche (*Wille zur Macht*) and the will to possession, which is the very stuff of individualism. But surely the other side of the coin of individualism, long exalted as the fulfillment of humankind, is egocentrism.

Subsequently, as Gabriel Marcel has shown, "having" has constantly gained supremacy over "being". As one's "having" mounts up, so one's "being" declines, and so does one's "readiness,"[4] which is the foundation of freedom. This leads Gabriel Marcel to state that "God has nothing, being everything," and "God is free."

Science is confronted with a problem (*pro-blema* – to place before). If we consider the case of the scientist and the object studied, we find a typical example of subject and object: 1) I, the scientist, observe, since the object of my investigations is outside of myself. Then, 2) I analyze, since I am outside the object. However, some things are inseparable; they cannot be placed before me because they form part of me; they are inside me. This is true of the soul, and even of the body. As Gabriel Marcel said, "my body is myself." But it can also be true of other people, if I love them. Love reveals the existence of self not as *Esse* but as *Co-Esse*; in other words, not as subjectivity but as intersubjectivity. This is how Gabriel Marcel attempts to define the existence of the "mystery," as distinct from the "problems" with which science is confronted.

This prompts us to ask the following question: "Does the human mind evolve at the same rate as natural science?" Do spiritual culture and the human sciences that study it evolve in the same way as the material civilization created by the natural sciences and their attendant technology? Many people think not, claiming that the human mind has not evolved since Greece; theology, ontology, metaphysics and everything that has been written since are mere transcriptions of what existed already.

I myself would say that the mind has regressed, or more precisely that it ceased to evolve when we gave reason supremacy over all the other human faculties. This took place in the seventeenth century, a hundred years after the discovery of the New World by the West – an event that stimulated thinking in every domain. Galileo and Descartes exemplify the spirit of the age. In succeeding centuries, the trend was confirmed by the success of the natural sciences as represented by such scholars as Newton, Pasteur, Mendel, Darwin and Edison, to name only a few. Hegel and then Marx gave their philosophical blessing at a late stage, like the owl of Minerva which takes wing at dusk. But these last failed to realize that they had merely followed in the footsteps of all the thinkers who had preceded them:

---

3. For a more comprehensive and positive view of Descartes' philosophy, see Chapter 6 above on "The Light of Reason" where we show that Descartes' total contribution transcends and outshines even his serious limitations. In fact, some of the "limitations" may be due to misreading – or non-reading! – of the original works of this genius.
4. Or, "availability"; *disponibilité* in Marcel's French.

they belong to a world that is Judeo-Christian in religion and Platonic-Christian in philosophy, in which the concept of linear time is well established and time has already given history its meaning. Without the convergence of "transcendence" and "immanence," history would not have existed. (Compare Kierkegaard's *Augenblick*, a radical transformative moment of insight and coping.)

That reminds me of a novel based on a story by Xuan Zhang, a wandering Chinese monk of the seventh century entitled "Journey to the West," which tells of a monkey-king (one of the monk's servants). To demonstrate his skills to his master, the monkey-king travels a thousand kilometers in an instant on a magic cloud. To prove this feat, he writes his name on the sheer cliff-face of a mountain at the other end of the world, and then returns. After listening patiently to the monkey-king boasting of his achievement, the monk shows him the palm of his hand on which he can see, written on the forefinger, the letters he thought he had inscribed on the distant mountain. In fact, the monkey-king had not traveled beyond the palm of the Buddha.

In propounding a philosophy that was meant to be all-embracing, Hegel did no more than travel within the palm of a hand – in his case, a Platonic-Christian palm: the Augustinian City of God (*Civitas Dei*). The heavenly city evolves in a particular direction and in linear time. For Hegel, the city becomes an earthly one, animated by *Geist*, within which he charts the mechanisms of the mind and the evolution of the world. Marx built on this by carrying the idea of "progress," viewed by him in increasingly material terms, to its utmost limits.

In the nineteenth century and on into the twentieth, belief in progress gave rise to the omnipotence of techno-science. As a result, a particular worldview gained prominence and eventually became universal, presumably because it spread with a momentum similar to the expansion of the West throughout the world. For 400 years, this vision has represented the one and only truth – truth here being necessarily scientific.

In the West, the tradition has gradually become fossilized after going through the transitional period in which the dichotomy between theological truth and scientific truth eventually became blurred, particularly in the aftermath of the French Revolution and the Industrial Revolution in the United Kingdom. And while the Church is still standing, a slow process of erosion is stealthily sapping its foundations.

This vision of the world, which might well have remained within the confines of the West, was disseminated throughout the globe on the heels of the phenomenon of western colonialist expansion. Here is the source of the problems of development: no development was conceivable unless based on the sole model of western development. The cultural identities of the colonized nations were marginalized if not spurned. It was then that the concept of the "East" emerged in counterpoise to the West. It is a concept that has no meaning in isolation; it exists only in relation to the West and might more accurately be termed the "non-West".

The real tragedy of underdevelopment is not so much economic in origin as the outcome of a spiritual submission: the cultural values of the peoples who had preserved their traditions were subordinated to the values of those who had lost them.

For a long time we believed in this kind of development, but today enlightened minds are beginning to recognize that all this has brought our planet to the brink of destruction. The non-West, submissive for so long, began to react after the 1970s. Unfortunately, this reaction often took a violent turn, with fundamentalism as one of the all-too-familiar examples. André Malraux predicted that the twenty-first century would be the century of culture, but, if present trends continue, it is more likely to be the century of cultural conflict.

And yet there were precursors in the West who realized that the vision peculiar to the North, regarded as universal, was in fact only a half-truth; these thinkers, foremost among them Goethe, recognized that there were other kinds of "knowing."

Jakob Boehme, Eckhart and also Haeckel, a pure scientist, had a deep respect for the beauty and order of nature. And what of Pascal, who said, "There is a logic of the heart as well as a logic of the intellect"?

Alexis Carel who, despite his Nobel Prize for medicine, did not enjoy the recognition of his peers for his work in the human sciences, explained very clearly the flaw in the western approach to reality. Here is his thought, as presented by Kiyoshi Inokuchi, a Japanese doctor. (The place references concern sites of UNESCO seminars, for which dates are supplied in a paragraph below.)

The disproportionate value attached to logical intelligence has distorted the human being as a whole.

My appreciation of Yujiro Nakamura for championing the "southern type of intelligence" (Venice) and of Ms. Kazuko Tsurumi for rehabilitating intuition (Balém) is attributable to the fact that I discern in Alexis Carel's system a basic pointer as to what we human beings should be. The mind can still evolve today, particularly if we are aware of the way in which human faculties have been distorted.

Paradoxically, a fundamental review of that world-view, based on deterministic science, has come from science itself, in particular quantum physics. From now on, the road to transdisciplinarity is open, as demonstrated at the seminars held by UNESCO in Venice (1986), Vancouver (1989), Paris (1991), Belém (1992), and recently Tokyo (1995).

It should be noted that, in addition to *intelligence-Logos (Ratio)*, which is "the most equitably shared thing of this world," to quote Descartes, the human faculties referred to by Alexis Carel relate to culture, or better still to the diversity of cultures.

"The task of transdisciplinarity is to engender a civilization on a planetary scale, which, strengthened by intercultural dialogue, embodies the individuality of each, and the wholeness of being." This statement is taken from the final

Unbalanced tendency of value system appearing in humanity today

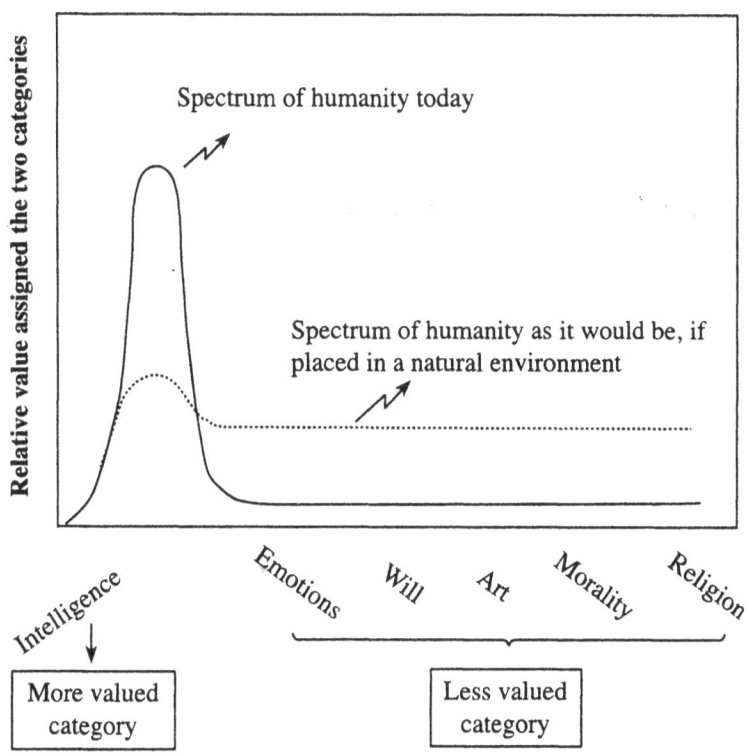

communiqué of the congress on "Science and Tradition: Transdisciplinary Perspectives, Openings to the 21st Century," held by UNESCO in December 1991.

Equally paradoxically, the discovery of the traditional values of Asia was made by western scholars: Nietzsche, Heidegger, Jung, Eliade and Lévi-Strauss among them. There are many who proclaim the excellence of the Veda or the Upanishads or who glorify Zen, in which the infinitely small is in direct communication with the infinitely large. But this appraisal of values requiring a comprehensive approach is still too often reached through cerebral reasoning.

One day, André Malraux, who relied more on his intuition than on his powers of reasoning, revealed to me the secret of his discovery of Japan. To my question: "When did you discover this difference between China and Japan?" he replied: "When I heard the sound of a Noh drum." And he discovered the vertical axis of Japanese civilization when contemplating the Nachi waterfall and strolling in the forest around the Shinto temple of Ise.

When I see the attraction exerted over western intellectuals by the cultural and spiritual values of Asia, I can only conclude that a process of reassessment is already under way – a reappraisal of the limits, if not the failure, of deterministic and mechanistic thinking and its roots. If the West may be defined as masculine, Asia is feminine to the extent that there the interactions between *Logos* and *Pathos*, between mind and body, are more apparent. The process may be interpreted as follows: a shift from the masculine to the feminine principle and from linear to circular time, the latter being peculiar to civilizations based on the feminine principle.

This brings us to a point at which formal Aristotelian logic is called into question, in particular the *principle of the excluded middle*. In western terms, the logic deriving from the all-round approach of Zen may be expressed as follows: A is A, and at the same time non-A. . . . To illustrate precisely: the One is itself the many, and the many the One according to the principle of the *included* middle.

It is a world in which the subject-object division disappears. It involves a return to the archetypal time of a great Unity before the birth of all parents (父母未生, *Fubo-Mishō*).

To achieve genuine transdisciplinarity, we need *transcultural* dialogue that is not just intellectual but that also takes into account artistic sensibility and bodily expression. We must develop a concrete, all-round approach to the "mystery" of others and of Being as a whole.

"*Genus humanum arte[5] et ratione vivit.*" It is through art (culture) and reason that we live a truly human life. In his address to UNESCO during his visit in June 1980, Pope John-Paul II quoted these words of Saint Thomas Aquinas: "Culture is a specific mode of 'existing' and 'being'." The pope then went on to say:

"Man who, in the visible world, is *the only ontic subject of culture*, is also *its only object and its end*. It is through culture that man as a human being becomes more human, 'exists' more fully and has more 'being'. And it is therein that the fundamental distinction between what man is and what he has, between being and having, is grounded. Culture is always essentially and necessarily related to what man is, while its relation to what he has, to his 'possessions,' is not only secondary, but entirely relative. . . . The experience of the different periods of history, not excluding the present, shows that we think about culture and speak about it *first and foremost in connection with human nature*, and only *secondarily and indirectly, in connection with the world of human production.*"

The pope rounded out his thought with these words:

"It is *in the unity* of culture as the distinctive mode of human existence that the plurality of cultures within which people live is rooted. Within this plurality, man develops without, however, losing the essential contact with the unity of

---

5. From Latin *ars*. The word covers the trades, professions, arts, occupations, jurisprudence and rhetoric, including dialectics. It can also refer to conduct, character, and cunning! (Cassell's Latin Dictionary, 1901)

culture as a basic and essential dimension of his existence and his being."

"UNESCO must become a world transdisciplinary forum," Mr. Federico Mayor, Director-General of UNESCO, told 1,500 delegates of Member States to the General Conference in October 1991. That forum will be the seat of transcultural dialogue in which respect for others will prevail and, not content with analysis and intellectual understanding, we shall seek a way forward by a concrete approach (to use the vocabulary of Gabriel Marcel).

Only a living tradition is worthy of the name. Cultural identity is not an object to be kept in a museum. A concrete, all-round approach to the cultures of others is the way to vivify one's own culture and identity. Experience will show that the dialogue of cultures is not merely desirable, but vital. With Lévi-Strauss, we maintain that: "Our only hope is the meeting and collaboration of cultures." In this way, humanity can regain the *Sapientia* left to languish in the shadow of *Scientia*. This is the way to a "community of minds," for the sake of our planet's future.

Bridge 36

When my pessimism goes unbridled, here's the way I feel: "If there is such a thing as a death wish, humanity right now is manifesting it collectively and mindlessly." This kind of feeling leads me to make some directed comments:

Eiji, you seem to have a capacity for realism and even-handed criticism of countries and cultures that is elevated by hope and a rationally compassionate spirit. You are a restorative for humanity's mind. That why I have been willing to give about a decade of my "golden years" to translating, thinking about, and conversing with you and others about this book. Your approach resonates with other writers I've recently learned to appreciate. . . .

Dear **Reader**, I can without reservation recommend two books that share the high excitement of adventure stories. Both illustrate Marcel and Hattori's "concrete approach."

The books are Dominique Lapierre's *City of Joy* (1985) and Greg Mortenson's *Three Cups of Tea* (2006-07). The first exudes the best of Franco-American culture as it encounters a multicultural miracle. *Three Cups of Tea* blends American and Pakistani ways of alleviating the deprivation and pain of women and children with the compassion of a famed Himalayan Mountain climber Mortenson. He once failed to reach a peak, but his "failure" allowed him to meet new friends who were embarrassed and discouraged about their children's lack of a schoolhouse (though the children worked hard to learn in an open air school of sorts, on some days lacking even a teacher). In helping villagers build the school for their boys and girls Mortenson benefited from these people's courage, wisdom and dignity.

National leaders, military figures, or even "terrorists" who read either of my recommended books run the risk of transforming their whole outlook on humanity's grief. That might even be the prelude to different ways of acting!

The crises mentioned in our book are overwhelming unless we are willing to seek out, deeply encounter, and emulate the right individuals. Thoughtful communion with a person or another culture or religion can outshine the darkness of any crisis. So, to sum up:

> Let's All Cross the Bridge the Other Way
> To where a "Firefly Glow" Leads Us

I owe it to readers to point out that in Hattori's closing essay preceding my present comments, this thoroughly Japanese Professor has succeeded in explaining the transversal of values in almost 100% Euro-American terms. It would be even better than "nice" if Americans, in fact, representatives of any nationality, could also "cross to the other side" with similar grace.

When a gift-bringer crosses any bridge to another person or culture, some "dirt" from the point of origin is bound to adhere to the crosser's body, shoes, sandals, or bare feet – in fact to anything about the gift-bringer. One way to "shake" the dirt from oneself is first to bathe thoroughly as a newly-arrived guest should and then, as quickly as possible, to learn to use the best ways not to harm the unfamiliar terrain. Because of the respect and restraint of some alien visitors, their wary hosts have become fast friends even with uninvited guests; they've even come to receive with genuine gratitude gifts that would otherwise be set aside with scorn. If Hattori and I have not quite made it to the "other side" of the bridge on every issue, we've sought always to meet at least in the middle.

For my part as translator and coauthor, I've used bridges, fireflies, notes and dialogue as my means of "bathing" away the grime of ethnocentric bias. Such grime includes those unconscious prejudgments that, like pathogens not scrubbed away, make us sick and may even take on plague-sized proportions.

Leaving my metaphoric language for a moment, I turn to some straight talk from the Muslim side. Do you know about the open letter signed by 138 Muslim religious leaders? The Reverend Allen Polen, a United Methodist minister writing the guest editorial for the *Winfield Daily Courier* of October 27, 2007, called my attention to it. The letter "went to world Christian leaders this week. It calls for conversation and cooperation around the shared principles of love of God and one's neighbor." The signatories include "clerics, scholars, politicians and academics representing virtually every Muslim nation and varied forms of Islam...." This is a letter that crosses to the other side and bathes itself in the purifying waters of goodwill.

Polen's editorial also reports on a "Muslim immigrant from the West Bank and Springdale, Arkansas." He is the general contractor Fadil Bayyari who "helped a Jewish congregation build a new synagogue by waiving his fee." Bayyari said, "Abraham is our forefather. We're first cousins. How we got to hate each other is beyond me." Jeremy Hess, the building project coordinator who worked with Bayyari, felt inspired to say, "You can't judge anyone except by the character of who they are."

One synonym for "transversal" in English as it applies to cultural diversity, is "cross-cultural," but as Hattori uses the term it also has the more mathematical sense of intersecting lines of diversity. The intersections are points in common; but what happens at intersections is more important than location per se.

Originating or intersecting points, as we approach the infinitesimal, become like zero – *Mu* in Buddhist philosophy. Mu, in my judgment, is a form of creative emptiness similar to a cleared lot or a mammal's womb.

The ego along with its restricted "place" in geography or culture can vanish into apparent insignificance. It then becomes like nothing to the popular eye, a thing "of no account." However, as the ego vanishes into sacrificial other-concern, the Kingdom Dawns on Earth. . . .

Any dawning may be accompanied by clouds, rain, even destructive storms. This week one of our church members lost 100 trees to one of our Kansas storms, and my barber lost several hundred acres of his corn crop and had all the windows knocked out of his house. The hailstones descended like baseballs. In such crises, the neighbors may rush to help in such astounding numbers and ways that nobody remembers exactly who rendered what help. And it doesn't matter. . . .

Hattori and I offer our persistent readers and fellow-learners this benediction. *May hope shine for you even amidst devastation . . . . (Some destruction will transmogrify into Creation's Continuance!)*

The Authors

Eiji Hattori

During his UNESCO career, Eiji Hattori served in various capacities initiating such projects as "Dialogue between Science and Culture" and an "Integral Study of Silk Roads: Roads of Dialogue." In 1994 he became Advisor to the Director General of UNESCO and has continued to represent the organization in many countries, including Japan and nations of the Middle East. He has residences in both Japan and Paris. His academic center of activity is Reitaku University in the Tokyo area where he has served as professor; he is presently the Deputy Director of the Research Center for Moral Science there.

Fluent in Japanese, French, and English, Hattori's linguistic and comparative skills have earned him an academic reputation. One of his functions as a scholar activist is to promote Japanese-Islamic dialogue and long-range decision-making on behalf of global peace, activities firmly grounded in his research into transversal values in accordance with the reality and growth of Dialogues among Civilizations. *Transversal* means integrally across (*trans-*) a resonance of values of the different civilizations, in contrast to universal, which too often exalts intellectualized science as the ONE value that dominates the arts, religion and every other function of humanity. "Transversal" refers to the depth of unity rather than its dominance.

Wallace Gray

As Kirk Professor of Philosophy, Wallace Gray taught for forty years at Southwestern College in Kansas and in 1997-98 as visiting professor at Kitakyushu University, Japan. His initiation into comparative studies took place at the East-West Philosophy Conferences at the University of Hawaii and the East-West Center. Both Gray and Hattori are widely published in several languages.

www.ingramcontent.com/pod-product-compliance
Lightning Source LLC
Chambersburg PA
CBHW021406290426
44108CB00010B/406